HOPE OR HINDRANCE?
THE CHURCH OF THE FUTURE

Hope or Hindrance?
THE CHURCH OF THE FUTURE

by ROSARIO SCARPATI

translated by Alba Zizzamia

SHEED AND WARD : NEW YORK

To P.C.

Foreword

THESE REFLECTIONS are the fruit of several years' work and countless exchanges of ideas with Italian and other friends who have different cultural backgrounds. We can claim that the changes now taking place in the Church and the widespread desire to be their conscious protagonists have justified both our encounters and the publication of this book. With it goes the hope that it will stimulate its readers—above all, those among them who have the inmost desire to refine and strengthen their religious loyalty.

I express sincere gratitude to my Italian and other friends who, as experts in religious sociology, have encouraged me to discuss these ideas on so many occasions. I am also very grateful to Father Camillo de Piaz, who helped me to complete the final version.

R.S.

Contents

Time in its aging course
teaches all things.
(Aeschylus, *Prometheus Bound*)

HOPE OR HINDRANCE?
THE CHURCH OF THE FUTURE

The Self-knowledge of the Church

THE CHURCH—a religious community, the People of God on pilgrimage to the end of time—possesses self-knowledge. This fact is evident in the Church's teaching, and it is presented in clear and pregnant synthesis in Pope Paul VI's encyclical *Ecclesiam Suam*.

Many contemporary theologians have pointed out the parallel between the psychological development of knowledge and the inner maturing of one's faith. Other scholars, moreover, speak of a social, or shared, knowledge of the religious experience of the group or community which accompanies the development of knowledge in society as a whole. It is in this context that the development of the Church's self-knowledge can be analyzed.

This is not to identify sociology with the science of society in Comtian terms. On the other hand, the last century undeniably witnessed an extensive diffusion of knowledge about man and his social relationships, so that we may say all life tends today to be viewed, posited, interpreted, and resolved in terms of a "social problem."[1]

Man's awareness of himself and his relations with others is the direct result of experience and is acquired by both the individual and the group from the capital present in society. The transfer of knowledge no longer takes place primarily through direct contact or relationships but through more impersonal, technical means which have become part and parcel of social custom. The shortened distances between peoples and unified techniques of communication offer new terms of comparison. The accelerated speed with which news, images, and experiences are transmitted—through economically profitable communications media—has immeasurably broadened the sociopsychological horizons of human experience. The dimensions of today's industrial, urban society, whose relations with outer space are already assured by a perfect relay system, the development of methods of data control and classification, specialized techniques for forecasts and projections—all of these have put at man's disposal an inexhaustible, and in certain sectors still untapped, mine of information on the organization of human life, resources, interactions, needs, and tensions. Before long this equipment will stretch its antenna into the past, and man will have a quantity of information on his immediate and remote history, only a minimal part of which he has been able to sketch to date.

All this is some indication of the flood of knowledge into which modern man is plunged in his search for identity and synthesis, and it is modern man who is a member of the Church as a religious community. The Church is composed of beings of this world—this modern world. The human condition cannot be extraneous to the Church if the Church is the continuation of the Incarnation. And by "the human condition" we mean human nature and the human person, psychologically and sociologically conditioned. Whatever is said of the Church inevitably includes whatever is said of man, precisely because he belongs to the Church and finds in the Church the instrument of his salvation *qua* man.

Since the Church is a religious, in fact a theandric, community, its self-knowledge will obviously differ in many respects from that of society or of a particular human group; but it cannot escape the laws of social knowledge, for these reflect the existential condition of man as a being in time. We can, therefore, analyze the progressive development of the Church's self-knowledge by concentrating on the religious truth it elaborates and expresses and the conclusions it draws from the religious experience of its members. This is a convenient distinction, for it differentiates religious knowledge in itself—which is notional and intellectual—from religious experience, which can be analyzed conceptually.

Tradition has accustomed us to this type of dissection, the heuristic and expository nature of which is too often forgotten. No religious truth is a discipline to be taught. If it is a religious truth, it is already a guiding principle of life. There is no orthodoxy which is not orthopraxy. Christianity is first a Person and then a doctrine.

These are useful observations to keep in mind. How far even venerable theological distinctions can go is illustrated by the fact that for centuries the need for orderly exposition led to

emphasis on a threefold division of the power of the Church
—teaching, government, and sanctification—whereas it is one,
sole, salvific power.

The proclamation of the Kingdom by Jesus and the formation of
the disciples are indissolubly linked to the Paschal Mystery in the
concrete economy of Redemption. It is here that ambiguous language is often found in theological works wherein Christ as priest
is distinguished from Christ as prophet and Christ as king. It is
obviously in keeping with tradition to say that our Lord is priest,
prophet, and king. The use of these titles to indicate separate
functions has permitted a convenient differentiation of the "powers"
of the Church in treatises *de Ecclesia*. But this differentiation,
which formalizes the Scriptural phrases, also contains a seed of
error insofar as it seems to imply that the Christian priesthood, as
such, is a purely cultural and sacrificial function and does not include the prophetic role or the governance of the faithful. . . . In
reality, there is fundamentally only one priestly "function," one
mediation, defined, like every function, by its object: the faith,
conversion to Christ, the Lord and Savior, in the union of the
People of God with the Sacrifice of the New Covenant. What are
commonly called functions are none other than the instrumentalities
derived from those which Christ received from the Father, the
union of which is necessary in order that the priestly ministry may
fulfil its mission to save the world through the faith and the
sacraments of the faith.[2]

In practice, such distinctions produced a series of ambiguities
in the conception and even in the theology of the priesthood,
and particularly in the formulation of the religious duty of

the laity, a general revision of which has been set in motion
by Vatican Council II. If, in this analysis of the change taking
place in the self-knowledge of the Church, we occasionally
use distinctions for heuristic or expository reasons, we have no
intention of pushing them to exaggerated conclusions, such
as accepting a development of dogma that is not an expression
—however incomplete—of the development of the religious
experience of the Christian community.

As our point of departure, we may take St. Paul's *Hoc enim
sentite in vobis quod est in Christo Jesu* ("Have this mind in
you which was also in Christ Jesus") [Phil 2:5]. Christianity
is feeling with Christ, consenting to Christ, acting in Christ
and through Christ.

The eminent theologian Emile Mersch starts with the consciousness of Christ and the reasons that this, along with the
consciousness of the faithful, constitutes the true unity of
sacred knowledge and, therefore, of the knowledge which
the Church—i.e., the faithful in Christ and with Christ—has
of itself. Writes Father Mersch:

The notion of consciousness is connected with the notion of being.
A being is knowable and knowing in the measure that it is in
act. To be conscious, then, is the same as to be. But it is such by
being so powerful that in virtue of it a person is himself for himself and possesses his own proper being in himself merely by
being. . . .

This close connection with being shows how consciousness can
have the first place in knowledge: it is first inasmuch as knowledge
is an apprehending by a knowing subject, a possessing by the

subject. For two aspects are distinguishable in knowledge: the act of grasping elicited by the subject, and the object that is grasped. In virtue of the first aspect, knowledge is subjective and interior, a personal thing terminating in the person; in virtue of the second, it is essentially objective, an apprehension of being as being.

The more perfect knowledge is, the more these two aspects tend towards complete identity. But one always supposes the other. Knowledge of being, hence true knowledge, is impossible without self-knowledge. . . . The converse is also true: genuine consciousness, true knowledge of oneself, is impossible without true knowledge of being as being. If anyone does not know his own person as a being he cannot claim to know it as it is, and therefore cannot claim to know it at all. Because of its close connection with being and with knowledge, consciousness is analogous, just as being and as knowledge are. Accordingly, there will be as many different types of consciousness as there are different types of being. As there is only one Being that exists fully, there is only one Being that is fully conscious. . . .

Since Christ is but one person, there is in Him only one consciousness, one ego, one subject that is the point of departure of all His acts and is the ultimate terminus of attribution. Consequently, there is only one who is conscious in Christ. But since this one who is conscious has two natures and two intellects, He has also two powers of saying "I," and in this sense He has a twofold consciousness. Each of these powers forms in Him a notion, or the equivalent of a notion, representing the "I," and thus Christ has two ways of expressing "I," or two expressions of consciousness.

The consciousness of Christ to be considered here is that belonging to Him as the first principle in the supernatural order, as the principle of unity in Christian teaching, as mediator; that is, the consciousness He has as a man: His human consciousness. . . .[3]

The self-knowledge of the Church, as the Mystical Body of Christ, lies in the awareness its members have in the whole Christ. If Christians are members of Christ, they must be, in the degree proper to members, what he is as head. The primacy which Christ possesses in the order of unity, intelligibility, and the grasp of knowledge that develops within consciousness, he transfers to his members; for he communicates himself to them in such a way that they, living his life, become sharers of his primacy.

Christians truly possess all that is needed to understand mysteries in the measure in which they are understandable here below. . . . This is because Christians, by the grace of God, are products of mystery, as Christ is; they are products of mystery in their faculty of comprehension, in their act of understanding and in their consciousness which, like all that they are, is from Christ and in Christ. . . .

Thus the unity of the whole Christ, which pervades all Christian teaching, also pervades the entire Christian organism that accepts it on faith. . . . The same unity is the reason why every Christian and his consciousness, in constituting the whole Christ in the manner proper to members, likewise constitute the unity of doctrine and its totality in the manner proper to members.[4]

Since the Church's self-awareness consists in the shared knowledge of Christ—the beginning and the end of the awareness of its members—communicated to the faithful at different times and in different situations, it is necessarily historical and progressive. The development of dogma, which takes place and can take place only in time, is one of its most formal expressions. This sense of progress in theological knowledge and in the formulation of dogma—and, therefore, fundamentally in the consciousness of the Church as a community—was underlined in *Ecclesiam Suam* and was clearly established in the patrimony of the Church at the Ecumenical Council.

Vatican Council II is the first council to affirm the evolution of Tradition, which it did in the Constitution on Divine Revelation. While previous councils dealt indirectly with the evolution of dogma, they were primarily concerned with its immutability, its unchangeableness in the evolutionary process. This Council, on the other hand, shifted the emphasis to its historicity; the faith remains always and identically the same, but in a dynamic and historical way.[5]

Here is where it is useful to distinguish between religious knowledge in itself and conceptual reflection on religious experience—in other words, between the knowledge which is proclaimed and the social consciousness which is something quite beyond and different from dogma *sic et simpliciter*. In sociological terms, we could express this as the development of social knowledge, shared through a social organism, and the evolution of the awareness of belonging to a social group.

Dogma expresses, in a normative but inadequate and fragmentary manner, Christ's knowledge of the mystery of God, communicated to the faithful in different historical situations. This does not mean that dogma lacks unity, for it subsists only to the degree that it is organic, that it is an integral deepening and explication of itself.

In Revelation-Word, the Church merely clarifies for the benefit of all mankind the reality of the absolute presence of the Mystery in Christ. She proclaims that this Mystery has come to us not only in a mystical, interior intimacy but also in historical, tangible and visible form. This fundamental statement sums up the whole kerygma and all Christian dogma, from the Trinity and the Incarnation to the life of grace and the Church with her ministry, worship, preaching, and sacraments and with the eschatological end of the individual and society. Revelation-Word, of which the Church is the organ, only makes explicit the implications of the absolute and gratuitous presence which, as Revelation-Reality, existed in the life of man even before his historical encounter with the Church-phenomenon. In addition, the free acceptance of this absolute, gratuitous presence of the Mystery is the very substance of what is called theological faith. To believe means to have faith in this present Mystery, to abandon oneself to it despite everything and in all circumstances. This statement, it seems to me, is of capital importance, since it implies that the acceptance of human existence with all its responsibilities is, in fact, an act of theological faith; for Christ, by living it, has shown us that human existence— not in the abstract but concretely—was for him—precisely in his human condition, which was immersed in the Mystery—the objective expression of his communion with the Father in the *dynamis* of the Holy Spirit for the benefit of his fellowmen.[6]

For this profound reason, the historical formulation of dogma is related to the degree of religious awareness and the type of formal expression man has arrived at in the various stages of his approach to the Mystery in actual life. For the same reason, the historical formulation of dogma obeys

a law of "opportunity" and, therefore, is necessarily progressive
in relation to the universal and absolute truth which will be
revealed in heaven. Without this vision of the instrumental
and partial but irreplaceable and necessary function of dogma,
we are reduced to static contemplation of its terms and complicated elaboration of dialectic analogies or to withdrawal in
proud rejection of all that is human and provisional in the
faith, thereby reducing it to something it is not: an arid syl-
logism of propositions detached from time and tied into the
juridical framework of a social body through a mysterious
series of dosages of authority.

Similarly, conceptual reflection on religious experience, the
awareness therefore of belonging to the religious group—
produced by life in common, a fixed type of institutional relationships, the collective representations that have been developed, and the social memory of the group—is subject to certain
psychological and sociological conditionings and to concrete
situations in human life. It is in this connection that the direct
relationship between historical and absolute truth and the
twofold understanding of tradition become apparent. As Schillebeeckx states, "the essence of the Church is manifest only in
historical and evolutionary movement."

We must avoid the dangerous inability to see the twofold
dimension of the one indivisible truth: the absolute which is
revealed only in a prominent historical movement and the
fact that historical truth reveals itself in speculative truth.
Christianity is not merely an ideology, a system of doctrine,
but an Event in which the history of salvation is accomplished.
Revelation, and therefore truth, is not only or principally the

communication of a body of truths which transcend human reason; it is, above all, the history of salvation, illumined by the prophetic Word, an Event which gives this history a beginning, a development, and an eschatological end in the epiphany, or manifestation, of the man Jesus, the son of God, the "perfector of the faith." Tradition is not an oral, conceptualist transmission of doctrine, but the living transmission of the reality of salvation itself.

All of human history is an integral part, and therefore a theological component, of the faith, which is lived, and of the consciousness of Christ imparted to the faithful. Psychology and sociology become, in a certain sense, part of the *scientia fidei,* lighting its progress with positive reflection. It is in this sense, I think, that Wach maintains that the sociology of religion must concentrate on the way a particular religious group interprets itself. With respect to Revelation-Word, the Church (i.e., the group) interprets itself in explicit and solemn manner through a competent body; with respect to Revelation-Life, this interpretation occurs through individual or collective reflection, communicated to all through different channels and charisms.

The consciousness of belonging, which can and must be expressed in visible, external, institutional forms, becomes fixed in the psychology of the individual and in the social memory of the group, according to the process of socialization by which the individual assumes his role and exercises it with varying degrees of awareness and responsibility, subject to conditionings which allow limited but real scope for the exercise of freedom. The sense of communion characteristic of the Church is expressed within the continuity and variety of temporal history, and our collective past is buried in the subconscious of each individual and of all society.

This existential reality cannot fail to be reflected in the self-knowledge of the Church—as is exemplified in the evolution of moral sense. This has been progressively refined (even to the point of exaggerated legalism) not so much or only because the urgency of its witness in the early days of the Church gave strength and endurance to generous souls but mainly because there has been slowly deposited in the collective subconscious of mankind a sharper sense of individual responsibility for one's actions—a responsibility centered on the true focal point of reference, namely, the human person in his relation to God and to his fellowmen.

We conclude, therefore, that we can and must apply to the evolution of the religious consciousness of a community, and consequently of the Church, the heuristic tools of the sociology of knowledge. The special nature of the Church and the particular origin of the revealed "datum" do not permit a plain and simple parallel—in content or method—with the general sociological approach in this field, which in any event has been explored only recently. Affirmations require great prudence, and analyses cannot be made lightly. If theology has had for some time the courage to tackle the history of dogma, it has not yet found the way to formulate a "sociology of dogma." In any case, when we speak of the reflective knowledge of the religious experience of a human group, we rightly inquire into the social and cultural bases of its thought system. We conclude, especially if this group is the Church, that if we cannot identify these bases with those of other systems, we must nevertheless admit that its mental products are related to a "historical situation," to a certain definable spiritual orientation and specific mentality. In this connection it is easy to recall the whole current of exegesis which formed the psychological and sociological mold of the Jewish mentality at the time of Christ in order to understand both the hold which tradition had on their expectations and the intellectual leap required to accept the "novelty" of Christianity.

The same procedure, with proper adaptation of method, might also be applied to the history of dogmas. In other words, the distinction is quite clear between the material and the formal object of the faith which has *per se* another kind of "basis," even if it is expressed in and by man. Other beliefs, survivals of the past, the later emphases given them, and those explanations of the faith which are not dogmatic in themselves but respond to some exigency in a particular historical situation—all are more or less relative and derive either from unofficial groups, from the laity or the clergy, or from ecclesiastical authority itself at a given historical moment. The study of the latent or manifest functions in a group, and of the structures it creates or uses in the conscious elaboration of certain collective concepts, falls within the same category. Think of the importance assumed by certain expressions—such as *Filioque,* in the centuries of dispute between Latins and Greeks—and then of the series of quite different meanings these expressions acquired as they became weighted in time with all the sociological burden characteristic of human groups in conflict.

Much of what is called the "opportunity" of a definition

could be analyzed, without loss of respect for or adherence to
the truth which it defines, by proceeding with a series of questions: To what extent has a particular teaching been dictated
by the need to ensure the stability of a cultural system, or even
of a broader social system, into which the Church has been
inserted? To what degree can it be said that a proclaimed
truth is or has been reduced to a defensive function to stave
off a crisis? What has been or is the degree of influence exercised by the historical situation in stimulating the explication
of a given teaching and in justifying it for the members of the
group and for others as well? These questions have not been
evaded by the more enlightened theologians, but what has
been lacking is the application of analysis and theological
conviction to groups and individuals, interests and ideals, crises
and hopes, in concrete life situations, so that the consciousness
of belonging might be clear and evident in the whole purify-
ing evolution and dialectically operative within a well-defined
historical period. Watching developments at Vatican Council
II has been, for the average Christian, perhaps the most interesting phase of his experience with this aspect of the Church
and also, for the first time, the most conscious, since the work
of the Council was public, concentrated more on concrete
questions of power and action, and hence more "pastoral."
The need now is to make this a widespread social custom,
almost a method of permanent self-examination. And related
to this is the need for public opinion in the Church.

Analysis must also be applied to collective judgments. It is
argued that experience and intuition can be collective, but that
judgment is always an individual matter both because it is the

result of reflection (which is an individual act) and because it finds expression in speech (and there is no collective organ for speech). Gurvitch maintains, however, that there is a collective element in the criteria for judgment, in the act of judging, and in the expression of judgment in words.[7] With respect to knowledge in the Church, it is of interest to pursue this subject more deeply, not so much for the analysis of the way the collective element enters the expression of judgment through "corporate techniques," which also produce the expressions of the group, but rather for an analysis of what in the Church is constitutionally a collective organ for the word: the magisterium.

Collective experiences and intuitions are subject to all the phenomenological variations and, therefore, are related to the sociocultural systems which permit their formulation and expression, even through legend and fable. There has not been sufficient study of how—or whether—there can be collective judgments which form the basis for specific adherence to a group through the sociological existence of a collective organ of the word. Certainly the magisterium of the Church cannot be considered a response to external pressure, by "corporate techniques," for social objectives, even though the traditional distinctions between *norma fidei* and the formulation of the object of faith, between subject and object of the magisterium, should be subjected to this type of analysis.

This brief digression on collective judgments as the basis for adherence to a group—and, consequently, on the role played at different times by their "diffusion," and on the capacity of individuals to interiorize these judgments and to

collaborate in their development—confirms the need to distinguish the essential from what is accessory, the permanent from
what is variable, in the self-awareness of the Church. It stands
to reason that the whole issue of the "philosophy of religion"
and the rational criticism of religious categories should be
viewed in this perspective. But there are other observations to
be made on the subject. These concern the utilization by the
magisterium of the historical material provided by mankind's
millenary experience in thinking about itself and, conversely,
the historical importance this use has had in the way individuals and groups have understood the Church, belonged
to it, and been its active members.

Father Chenu writes:

The enunciation and origin of dogmas or infra-dogmatic beliefs,
in the faith of the believer and the Church-community which
regulates this faith, will be rendered theologically intelligible
through analysis of their content, conducted with all the resources
of the cognitive processes, whether these derive from the general
psychology of the individual, as in the analysis conducted by all
theology teachers, or whether they derive from the psychology of
the group in particular, if it is true that collective man is part of
the individual man. St. Thomas, in his *intellectus fidei,* used the
resources of Aristotelian, Augustinian, and other philosophies. If
philosophy today has explored as a new field the knowledge of
collective behavior . . . it is logical for the *intellectus fidei* to put
these new resources to use. Let us say also that the Catholic faith
finds therein a homogeneous connection, coessential with its own
intelligence, if it is true that for Catholicism there cannot be true
and justifying faith except through and in assent to the Church

as a community and as a society. For a theology filled with the assent of faith, this primacy of the community in the transmission and enunciation of faith is precisely the basis for recourse to knowledge of man's collective behavior where his feelings and especially his religious assents are concerned (e.g., the sociology of authority in "orthodoxy"). To borrow the language of the sociologists, religious phenomena, for the Christian, notwithstanding the irreducible personalism of interior faith (not only in mystical experience but in the elementary act of faith) are above all "social facts," not only because of the psychological conformity of orthodoxy or worship but in the very heart of their assent. Therein, theologically speaking, lies the mystery of the Church, the Body of Christ, animated by the Spirit. Faith in the communion of saints will find a remarkable intelligence in its "dogma" if it uses as the vehicle for this intelligence a psychology, a phenomenology, a philosophy of the community.[8]

As the same theologian observes elsewhere, Catholic theology, in its reaction against Protestantism (which dissociated faith from dogma, setting the interior inspiration of the Spirit against the teaching authority of the Church), placed so much emphasis on the role of the Church, not only with respect to the objective teaching of Revelation but also to the very conscience of the believer, that the faith came to seem increasingly an act of obedience to a rule, the definition of which Christ entrusted to the Church. "The faith adheres to a 'dogma.' And so a new theological meaning enters this ancient Greek word, which used to express a concept combining the intellectual aspect of truth and the juridical aspect of a decree."[9]

Before the Counter-Reformation no Christian had separated

external obedience to the Church from inner docility to the
Holy Spirit. However, and for historical reasons easy to understand, reaction to the Reformation led certain schools of
theology to impose, as it were, the testimony of the Church
on the interior act of faith—as if the dogmatic magisterium
was the formal motive for the believer's adherence. Thus,
through processes characteristic of a social body which establishes its own norms of conduct and determines the justifications for its actions, the Church ceased to be solely the qualified
depository of Revelation; it became the motive for acceptance
of the faith. If this intensified the feeling of community and
made it easier to identify and differentiate the religious group,
it failed to inspire to the same extent—because of the alternative
character of faith in the mystery of salvation—a consciously
voluntary participation.

Chenu continues:

Since then, it seemed the believer could be indifferent to the content of his faith since he belonged to this Church; or at least his
membership in the Church implied, without need for further
penetration into the heart of the matter, the acceptance of the
truths revealed by God: an implicit faith, it was said, would suffice
for one to live as a Christian even without knowledge of the
Incarnation of Christ or the existence of the Word of God. This
impoverishment of the object for the benefit of the teacher obviously produced a reversal of values in the mind of the believer.
Primary importance came to be accorded the acceptance of the
decrees of this Church-witness, obedience to its words, enrollment
in its organization. The first thing was to obey; the intimate
grasp of truth, the infused understanding which leads to the

knowledge of God, would come later. . . . There thus developed a religious mentality which became embodied in the teaching, in certain theological treatises, on the nature of the faith and the Church.[10]

In this way the original balance in the believer's psychology was gradually modified and, consequently, so were the social relations within the community of the faith. The structures set up to preserve the community in the faith and allow it to develop itself were devised and functioned in this mental climate. And since this mentality was static and sustained itself with historical methods of exercising the ministry of the word, it took the Council of Trent as its shield and support. The effects soon became apparent even in the way the Church explained the history of salvation in the most remote villages. The Church became an authority to which everything was entrusted and, in addition, the only authority for knowledge of the Church.

Since this authority had a sacral character (and this over and above the functions of ministry in the community), this knowledge became the patrimony of the hierarchy. It is always true that a type of knowledge of society and of the mechanisms which govern it accompanies power and the exercise of power. And it is also true that in a religious community the monopoly of knowledge, when reduced to norms expressed juridically or to a juridical posture, withers the sense of participation; furthermore, the monopoly not only assumes a sacred character but becomes shrouded in mystery. The first consequence of this is that truth becomes more a privilege to

be administered and bestowed than a self-diffusing good. In
the psychology of the believer, who is formed and socialized
in a certain way,

obedience becomes the specific feature of his perfection, and the
loving contemplation of the truth, the healthy curiosity of the
mind, must not be developed except with reservations and pre-
cautions. The faith is, first and foremost, orthodoxy. . . . Dogma
is a decree, and the faith is obedience. But decree and obedience are
only the condition—the essential condition, but only a condition
nevertheless—of the life which faith and dogma give, a foretaste of
the beatific life.[11]

In recent centuries this religious mentality influenced the
sense of belonging and the very process of identifying the religious object. This is not accusation, but factual judgment. We
must keep in mind a principle which excludes the sound and
admirable exceptions that have always existed and concentrate
on the progress of the social body as a community. According
to Max Scheler, the more abstract an idea, the more incapable
it is of exercising a dynamic influence on society. Ideas are not
realized, do not take on form and substance, until they are
somehow linked to the interests, impulses, emotions, and
tendencies of the community and until they are embodied in
institutional structures. Ideas which are not rooted in the
immanent development of real factors are destined to remain
sterile utopias. Now the Counter-Reformation was certainly a
real and popular movement. The ecclesiastical structures were,
and in many ways still are, fashioned to meet a real need. To

speak, therefore, of a particular mentality in the Church over the centuries is not an abstract idea, but an objective recognition of its manner of being, knowing, and acting. It is logical that this is where the greatest change should occur. To take note of the change and acknowledge it publicly—as happened in the Council—is an unmistakable sign that the Church can change with respect to its knowledge of itself, just as it is an objective fact that this new perception occurs at different levels and that the persons higher in the power structure are the most resistant to change. But the latter is not an argument to prove the Church cannot change. It merely confirms the fact that it is more difficult for it to change because the power structure is too closely bound up sociologically with the authority of the organ of the Word (magisterium) and the sacral character that has gradually been attributed to its members.

In practice, for the average Christian the obligation of obedience, inserted in the inner act of faith as the motive for the act, has had all the sociological conditions of group life to be reduced thereby to a mere juridical enrollment. Much of the crisis in many minds today is the result of a historical process whose beginnings are remote. Even the existence of crises, however, the discussions which they stimulate, the thinking which results—all march toward change. The most wonderful thing in the Church is precisely this clarification in action. It is not only a theological clarification, due chiefly to that theology wrongly called "new"; psychologically and sociologically, it is a clarification of awareness in the sense that the motives for adherence to the faith have become more mature among both clergy and faithful: a new religious mentality has been taking shape. The Council provided the occasion and the competence for its expression, but it must still find or establish new institutional forms.

Notes

[1] Cf. H. Hoefnagels, *La Sociologie Face aux Problèmes Sociaux* (Paris, 1962).

[2] L. Dingemans, "Dévaluation de la Fonction Sacerdotale," in *Evangéliser* (April 1965).

[3] E. Mersch, *The Theology of the Mystical Body* (St. Louis, Herder, 1951), pp. 76–78.

[4] *Ibid.*, p. 84.

[5] E. Schillebeeckx, *La Troisième Session du Vatican II,* Lecture held at DO-C, Rome, Nov. 12, 1964.

[6] E. Schillebeeckx, *L'Eglise et le Monde,* Lecture held at DO-C, Rome, Sept. 16, 1964.

[7] Cf. G. Gurvitch, *Traité de Sociologie,* Vol. II (Paris, Presses Universitaires de France, 1960), pp. 133–134.

[8] M. D. Chenu, *La Foi dans l'Intelligence* (Paris, 1964), pp. 64–65.

[9] *Ibid.*, p. 22.

[10] *Ibid.*, p. 23.

[11] *Ibid.*, pp. 24, 27.

TWO

The Church as
a Cultural Organism

THE CHURCH, as a cultural organism, can and does change, since development is a law essential to the faith which guides the Church and since man is in the process of evolving psychologically and sociologically even in his *intellectus fidei*. This process does not change the true nature of the Church, but deepens it. It is characteristic of the Church as a religious community and in all its manifestations. It links the Church to the broader whole of human evolution and constitutes not only a safeguard but also a stimulus and a direction toward higher goals.

EVOLUTION OF RELIGIOUS KNOWLEDGE

The changes that take place in the Church evolve with the development of religious knowledge in general. It is well to note that religion does not comprise the whole culture or

entire spiritual patrimony of a people, even though it is the
expression of their approach to the "divine" or "sacred." The
phenomenology of religion and the comparative history of
religions are based on this premise. There have been recent
attempts to develop a philosophy of religion that would, in
fact, formulate a criticism of religious categories so that the
specific content of religion, as the understanding of the divine,
would be clarified through and beyond individual and social
expressions of religion. This critical "purification" has not been
—and perhaps cannot be—carried to conclusion on the historical level. Nor can it be carried through on the philosophical
plane, since factual judgments on historical expressions of
religion are governed by canons which take for granted the
impossibility of grasping the general and universal content
of religion. Dualist, reductionist, and even phenomenologist
attempts have foundered on the recurrence of religious elements and traditional creeds. There is always something that
eludes analysis and voids conclusions. Atheism, as criticism,
presumes the existence of this "something"; as a value it takes
on the same significance. It is preferable, therefore, to proceed
on the historical level and to analyze how changes have
occurred in the Church as a result of the evolution of religious
knowledge in general.

Man unquestionably knows and recognizes God, whose
ontological attributes he describes according to the kind of
knowledge he has, the importance he gives to this knowledge
in his life and thinking, the terms he has developed and the
associations he has arrived at through reasoning about his

experience of nature and his fellowmen. This means that human consciousness is at the basis of religion and that man's membership in and relationship to the actual group among whose members he lives and in which he receives his first value judgments are determining factors in that consciousness. This is in no way an attempt at philosophical analysis of the essence of religion or psychological analysis of its interiorization. Philosophy today is slipping into phenomenology, while psychology accepts functionalism as an analytical method. "All recent theories on personality are to a certain extent functional,"[1] and personality itself has become "the dynamic organization in the individual of those psychological systems which decide his characteristic and original adaptation."[2]

With respect to religion, therefore, philosophy and psychology attempt to be free of genetic assumptions and to concentrate instead on the dynamics beyond the structural classifications arrived at in the past through the typological method. This entails the conscious risk of relativism, but it also means freedom from the hobbles imposed by a preconceived value system. In this connection, as in the case of the historical sciences, the relationship between the value judgment and the choice of object and method should be defined. This has not yet been done with sufficient clarity and precision.

In any case, it is correct to analyze, in the context of social dynamics, how changes in religious knowledge are related to specific social structures and how the latter are directly influenced by the evolution of all human thought. This enables us to understand the processes by which religious knowledge specifically manifests its presence and exerts a predominant influence in the group, how this is lost, and how the religious institution plays a determining role in this process.

Since any analysis of religious knowledge must inevitably refer to the cultural framework of the society under study, it is well to define the meaning of "culture."

Human behavior is not only influenced by a given economic system, is not only woven through the intricate pattern of relationships and institutions; it requires the justification of all existence, conformity to the common aims and ultimate goals of the society in which one lives. Every society, in fact, develops a system of symbols and expressions which epitomizes and harmonizes its beliefs, tastes, myths, and ideals and forms the matrix in which its institutions (in mutual cooperation and relationships) function as a total system. In other words, every society develops a culture. The individual's actions are regulated by norms, accepted types of behavior, criteria which imply a value system. On the basis of this value system, the individual arranges beliefs, actions, approval and disapproval, ideologies and ideals, moral laws and legal obligations in a certain hierarchical order, and his conduct reveals the cultural traits of the society or group to which he belongs. . . . In practice, the individual is conditioned by the cultural patterns of his environment; he follows certain specific modes of judgment, certain specific types of justification, and he either conforms to institutional rules or he ignores and rejects them. This means that his needs and his predispositions to act and to choose fall always within a frame of reference which is precisely the cultural one.[3]

It is no mystery that religion, which in itself embodies a hierarchy of values, makes a considerable contribution to this frame of reference. The contribution of religious knowledge to the development of the sciences, at least in establishing initial hypotheses, is also recognized. And, finally, there is the obvious contribution of religious knowledge to the development of cultural categories, precisely because of the sensitivity of religious knowledge to the divine, however inadequate and fragmentary is its expression in human terms.

Progress in the sciences—which always produces a change of perspective as to values—has, in turn, an impact on the world of religion and upsets some of its most stable and apparently secure positions. But "what makes this a favorable circumstance is precisely the rise of sociology (social psychology and its other branches), by reason not only of the conclusions arrived at in its inquiries in the field of religion . . . but also in the development of doctrinal categories which constitute its scaffolding."[4] The practical effect of this normal osmosis is observable in the above-mentioned attempt to work out a critical philosophy of religion, as well as in efforts to reexamine religious and theological categories in relation to the sociological, and vice versa.

From the foregoing it is easy to see how there can be different visions of the world and different forms of religious approach and knowledge. Father Pin writes:

In sociology, vision of the world is defined as the intellectual organization of the different elements comprising the particular world of an individual or a people. Such organization supposes, in the first place, a structural arrangement of the world: the subject distinguishes in his conscious universe a series of elements, parts, levels, categories, which, *acto secuto,* he must integrate into a coherent whole. This integration presupposes, in turn, a unifying principle which derives from the concept man forms of the absolute and its relation to the different, "anteriorly" distinct elements. When the absolute is conceived as a personal God, or at least as a more or less personal divinity, the vision of the world takes on a religious character.[5]

We may thus describe the elements which enter into different "visions" of the world according to how they are integrated by particular individuals, groups, or cultures at various stages of their development, both in time and in conscious reflection. It is then possible to trace an evolutionary process in the field of religion that is phenomenological in character and reflects this development, but does not involve a discussion of the essence or origin of religion itself. This is the most correct procedure and the framework in which to examine the evolution that has taken place in the Church in relation to the evolution of religious knowledge in general.

The doctrinal teaching and the experiences shared in a religious group do not take the place of the integration the individual accomplishes for himself or makes his own with the symbols and images common to a group or culture. It is known that beneath the surface of religion, as it is lived or practiced in the various churches or sects, there persist certain religious subcultures and certain personal amalgams of beliefs which, in the last analysis, govern the passage from faith to action. Since the Church is composed of individuals and groups, it is also the expression of this integration in their respective visions of the world, in addition to being the organ of a much higher level of integration through enlightenment from another source and with other contents, symbols, and social actions.

Moreover, the relationship between act and meaning, between word and mystery of the presence, especially in the liturgy, conforms not only to a revealed value and relationship but, precisely because of the fundamental mystery of the Incarnation, to the normal processes of psychological and sociological integration. In outlining the evolution of religion—which in a certain sense has influenced and been influenced by the religious knowledge of the Church, an interplay of influence that still continues—Bellah considers three levels of evolution:

The scheme is based on several presuppositions, the most basic of which [is] that religious symbolization of what Geertz calls "the general order of existence" tends to change over time, at least in some instances, in the direction of more differentiated, comprehensive, and in Weber's sense, more rationalized formulations. A second assumption is that conceptions of religious action, of the nature of the religious actor, of religious organization and of the place of religion in the society tend to change in ways systematically related to the changes in symbolization. A third assumption is that these several changes in the sphere of religion, which constitute what I mean by religious evolution, are related to a variety of other dimensions of change in other social spheres which define the general process of sociocultural evolution.[6]

Bellah posits five ideal typical stages of development, but he recognizes that there is no inevitability about these stages,

that there is a broad spectrum of types within each stage, and
that it is often impossible in actual cases to designate the
precise stage because of the presence of many extraneous
features:

Now, for heuristic purposes at least, it is also useful to assume
a series of stages which may be regarded as relatively stable
crystallizations of roughly the same order of complexity along a
number of different dimensions. I shall use five stages which, for
want of better terminology, I shall call primitive, archaic, historic,
early modern and modern. These stages are ideal types derived
from a theoretical formulation of the most generally observable
historical regularities; they are meant to have a temporal reference
but only in a very general sense.[7]

Since religious knowledge is related to existential factors, it
develops in time, and the degree to which its presence is felt
in society depends on the historical role of the religious institution which proclaims it or on the social groups which accept
it. A change in the Church is observable, therefore, by virtue
of this general evolution of religion and the part played by
religion in a given cultural framework. Change is also observable in the role the Church has played in specific areas
and cultures and in the life of certain communities, in the
Church's understanding and use of the social organ of the
word, in the means of communication it recognizes or mo-
nopolizes and the degree to which these are accepted by those
to whom they are addressed. An analysis of change thus leads
to an analysis of institutions; and given their role in human

history, this leads, in turn, to a general view of history. No change, of whatever kind, can be explained without attempting to explain the general context in which it occurred and without inquiring what its final goal is. In other words, it is impossible to analyze the meaning of change in a religious institution without reference to an eschatology. The Christian's belief is all the clearer since history is in a certain sense already ended, in that its premise has been fulfilled in the Incarnation. We are awaiting only the fullness of the Parousia through our inner participation in the *magnum mysterium* revealed and accomplished by Christ.

An example or two from history might help to clarify this aspect of the question. One of the most obvious transitions in the development of religious knowledge, the religious institution, and the groups which accepted it took place in the period between the *Summa Theologica* of the late Middle Ages and the separation and specialization of the various branches of learning. While retaining the concept of dualism between God and the world (of which man was a part), modern civilization created a new relationship between man and nature and thereby developed a new type of conscience in man and a new "nontheological" vision of nature. Consequently, on the sociopsychological level, religious knowledge was reduced to a restricted sphere of human experience. At the same time, a separation took place between practical knowledge and speculative knowledge, severing these two natural tendencies in man so that social efficiency became the almost exclusive province of science while religion was assigned specifically to the interior life. From a universal and uncontested presence, authoritative and generally widespread in all sectors of life, religion was reduced to a partial presence of limited diffusion, resisted, liberalized, with certain new and varied features.

Modern times adopted the scientific method as its objective criterion and rejected that of authority. The basic need for authority, however, left to the relativism of the various disciplines, made a religion of science—which, in principle and method, can neither be a religion nor assume its mantle of authority. Restricted to the interior life, religion became prey to sentimental exaggerations and accentuated a limited concept of man. As a result, it was either rejected, became a religion of the elite, or found expression in the most varied forms of animism and ritualism.

In this historical process, however, there occurred a certain purification, that is, religion became increasingly disassociated from the "sacred." If in certain geographical areas and in some cultures the "sacred" has undergone—and seems still to be undergoing—a kind of eclipse in direct relation to scientific and technical progress, religion has progressively divested itself of mystery and has come down to the essential relationship with the Absolute through the community of the faithful which is the Church. The true question, then, is whether the Church submitted to the change or whether it directly assumed the responsibility for this purification.

Father Chenu comments:

It is very true that scientific and technical progress, by reducing man's intellectual and creative impotence, eliminates the transference our ancestors made, through ignorance and fear, to the Divinity. To know and to seek to penetrate the causes of things risks having recourse no longer to the Supreme Cause. But this temptation and danger will not be dealt with unless there is first a desacralization which, in fact, purifies religion of coarse deviations and restores to it the transcendence that has been obscured by abusive recourse to the miraculous. God is not a stopgap for deficiencies in our knowledge of nature or social morality. Man's dominion over nature leads him to the true God.

Here, in fact, history is the witness. Every stage of progress, every era of civilization, brings with it—in contrast to animist religions—a transfer to the secular of whole areas—in science, human psychology, the concept of the family, social behavior, political power, group limits—previously endowed with so-called sacred values. The Christian still believes that authority comes from God, but he no longer consecrates kings. He still believes in the sanctity of the family, but he no longer venerates his ancestors. Thus Christianity, of all religions, desacralizes nature, including the social nature of man.

Christian civilization, in the strict sense of the word, was the result of religious compensation for a humanity which did not yet have the key to an earthly economy. Today we make a clear distinction between civilization and Christianization.[8]

In another discussion of these same concepts, Chenu adds:

The first law of scientific and technical rationalism is never to set a field apart *a priori* as being beyond hope of penetration, protected by mystery and prohibitions. Let nature be revealed, let man's mastery be accomplished, and faith will have its own domain in the enjoyment of its own object and with pleasure in the objects, the discoveries, the achievements of reason, which are the reflection of God. It is the relationship between the secular and the sacred which is under discussion and requires revision. For what is sacred can become secular, and what is secular can become sacred. The frontier is open. There is no objective principle which imposes a permanent division between secular and sacred things. The secular is in no way devalued, and much less is it culpable for being outside the sphere of immediate experience of God. To define these frontiers is the task of mankind's historical action. The age of technology is an occasion of this kind. By fostering the decline of a specific "sacredness," it contributes to the purity, the truth of "religious" knowledge.[9]

This historical process developed parallel to that which first reduced and then defined the role of religious institutions in general and the Church in particular. There is no need to stress here the positive effect of the end of the so-called "era of Constantine" and of the resultant evangelical image of the Church in the service of the world, conscious of its true function rather than a claimant of privileges from the State. With the general desacralization of culture, a revision of the hierarchy of values, and therefore of the role of institutions, was inevitable. It is precisely the evolution of some fundamental institutions under the pressure of technical progress that has led to a more composite pattern of social organization, a pluralistic society based on the acceptance of the democratic ideal. The Church has undergone a purification of great importance in the loss of temporal power—even though the temporal mentality persists in certain individuals and sectors of Church life. The Church's image is no longer one of power but of the permanent service of the Word of life and of sanctification. If today this image and conviction are becoming widespread, we must not forget that this has come about in recent times through conflict and dispute. The remnants of recent polemics obscure this positive fact, which is now a part of contemporary religious consciousness.

These two processes, which Bellah considers the transition from the compact to the differentiated, have also led to a refinement of religious knowledge in general. This has not failed to have beneficial effects—which will become increasingly clear —on culture as a whole. These observations, however, are restricted to a limited historical experience, that of Western culture. We too often forget the positive value of other cultures in this confrontation, especially those of the Orient. In this transitional period, especially in the last century, it was established practice to use outmoded categories to support the day-to-day dialectic. There has not been a true rational criticism which could preserve, along with the logical and heuristic value of such categories, a certain unity of knowledge. Consequently, religious knowledge has suffered more than other forms from the "alienation" of the sciences. Its castle of logic, the fruit of centuries of reflection, has been shattered, both in the psychology of the believer and in the cultural functions of society in general.

It is undoubtedly true that human thought has discovered the value of pluralistic knowledge, has explored new fields, and has uncovered new methods and new conditionings. But it is also true that it has lost its sense of unity in one final destiny and has sensed the disappearance of its deepest ethical motivations, which were linked to the old logic. Consequently, it has sought its justifications in other objects and fields of reality, outside itself, in a kind of self-alienation and prostitution to the object. The contacts between man and nature and man and his fellowmen were lost.

The state of mind, the state of society is of a piece. When we discard the test of fact in what a star is, we discard it in what a man is. A society holds together by the respect which man gives to man; it fails in fact, it falls apart into groups of fear and power, when its concept of man is false. We find the drive which makes a society stable in the search for what makes us men. This is a search which never ends; to end it is to freeze the concept of man in a caricature beyond correction, as the societies of caste and master-race have done.[10]

The decline of values in the sciences was reflected in the inner struggle that beset scientists when confronted with the most fearsome of alternatives, nuclear war and the extinction of the human race. They thus rediscovered ethical imperatives and began to retravel the religious road they had abandoned.

The Church as a religious institution, composed as it is of human beings who need hard experience and painful conflict to awaken them to their responsibilities, was very late in re-establishing the dialogue with secular culture in general and with the science of religion in particular. The Church had accumulated too many centuries of privilege, and its heritage of fidelity to the Word, of which it is the organ and witness in the world, was too precious. Furthermore, religious learning had been restricted, as in the case of theology, to ecclesiastics and gradually became their exclusive preserve. When the break came, there was already a separation between the general mass of people and the learned classes; and struggles for other ends and purposes had already impoverished the common ground on which group consensus had flourished, namely, the catechism and the *biblia pauperum*. From the time of the Scholastics, training methods in the Church lacked systematic organization, although they corresponded to local needs; and, above all, there were none of the *aggiornamenti* which change demanded.

If the Counter-Reformation produced a spiritual awakening, thanks to the current of reform always alive in the Church and which indeed served as a lever for the "protest," if the disciplinary decrees of the Council of Trent led to the establishment of the parish and the seminary as permanent institutions, and if the catechism represented the true new *Summa* of the times, then the role of the Church as an institution, as the guarantor and interpreter of religious knowledge in the whole domain of learning, was no longer the same. The theological mentality was closed to the new orientation and new historical situation. The defense of tradition often became a prejudged rejection of change. The emphasis on the Church and the definitions which today seem so incomplete exhausted the effort at conciliation in the field of ecclesiastical learning, or rather theology, and ignored the whole body of religious learning contained in the new cultures appearing on the Western scene through geographical discoveries. After the efforts of the first great pioneers, missionary activity, remarkable and in many respects miraculous as it was, developed in ways that were often offensive and failed to take into account the values inherent in the local religions. The privileged possession of a distilled philosophy, attained with great losses even in the West, prompted an instinctive disesteem for the great religions encountered, because they were too laden with myths, pervaded by animism, and burdened with primitive rituals. The conflict therefore—since there was no contact—arose between theology and science. The role of the Church as interpreter of the *anima naturaliter Christiana* was thought to be accomplished and was taken for granted when it was not completely neglected.

In this historical process the secularization of learning and consequent "reduction" of religious sciences and institutions did not, however, lead solely to negative results, as is often thought. The purification of religious knowledge had its impact on the self-awareness which the Church was acquiring in modern times. It can be truly stated that all the movements for revision, both in the language and in the whole activity of the Church as a cultural system, contributed to the secularization of culture and that, as serious students of the subject have observed, atheism represents a dialectic element of religious purity with respect to both knowledge and life. To quote Father Chenu again, "Atheism is a tragic threat; but to assess and overcome it, we must not attribute to de-Christianization what is a normal consequence of the desacralization of the various structures—scientific, economic, political, ideological—

of a human society now guided by its laws in the organization of nature." [11]

In this sense, while the massive phenomenon of communism has generated in the Church the inevitable defense reactions against totalitarianism, it has also revived the natural appeal of religion and has unquestionably inspired recent ecclesiastical policy to move in other directions in some sectors. The Council secretariats for Christian Unity and for Non-Christian Religions are a recognition of this trend, which is one that awakens a new type of awareness. Despite all this, however, we must admit that we are faced with a tragic situation: science in search of values, and widespread religious awareness in search of modern expression. Here the consciousness of the Church becomes the crossroad of the world of thought. The Church's position is not one of imperial authority guaranteed by the privilege of truth, but one of responsibility that can be borne only by the incentive of faith and the support of a living tradition.

PROGRESSIVE SELF-KNOWLEDGE OF THE WORLD

From the foregoing it is evident that the Church, set in the world as living leaven, changes according to the knowledge which the world progressively acquires of itself. We have noted how scientific developments have had and continue to have an influence, however indirect, on theology. Historically, this influence has often taken the form of opposition or conflict, it has frequently polarized around particular positions, and it has sometimes been manifested with high drama; but it is no longer questioned. Even determinism grants not only the interdependence and close relationship between ideologies (which it views as superstructures) and the economic bases of society but, even to a greater extent, the interrelationships among the ideological sectors themselves.

To arrive at the true *intellectus fidei*, we can, by way of analogy, take as our starting point the use of categories proper to the different disciplines. This use is perforce related to the progress within the disciplines themselves and to the awareness of their methods, limits, interrelationships, which men acquire in the course of time. It is precisely in this particular period of awareness that one of the most interesting aspects of the change in the Church as a cultural system is to be noted: that is, the Church changes in relation to the role and social function of the knowledge which the world acquires of itself, and it does so in the broadest historical range of human experience.

The world has become progressively aware that it is an autonomous value in itself, and today this awareness is growing almost automatically. In this process it is possible to discern specific values and tensions, but to be noted especially is the increasingly evident and widespread tendency to greater freedom as a permanent condition of man vis-à-vis the cosmos, society, and his own consciousness. The natural sciences have revealed with increasing clarity that the world is not stifled by necessity but, rather, is permeated by a purpose, by a reaching upward. The concept of law directly related to and modeled on the law of nature, which used to be expressed in mechanistic constants, has been revolutionized. The principle of relativity has released the natural sciences from the shoals of the compelling absolute, sent them off into relative times and spaces, and demonstrated that all such laws are statistics. Hence the principle of indetermination has introduced the unforeseeable into the real, not as a determining cause, but in the sense that man's intelligence and the practical applications of his knowledge cannot possibly be determining factors even with all the powerful computers and artificial antennae at his disposal. While mathematics has perfected the tools for making forecasts and projections, it has also developed a pattern that is the more perfect as it is the more incomplete with respect to the whole of human experience. Working definitions have become the hypotheses which serve as starting points for the experimental sciences, given the inadequacy of the traditional tools of logic and philosophical definition.

In this ferment of relativity, mysterious acceleration of elements, and unsuspected cycles, there has emerged, in different sectors and with sometimes conflicting methodologies, a kind of new "soul of the world." This "soul" is not so much a formal element that determines and gathers all of reality with its different degrees of analogy and causality into an organic whole, but rather a kind of dynamic equilibrium which exists because of the thrust of all elements toward qualitatively superior goals of evolution.

This equilibrium is not the homogeneous result of an archetype to be realized later or in the process of realization. It is, rather, the permanent and necessary historical ambience for the actualization of a richer and more complex level of reality itself.

Within this natural framework the world or cosmos seems, indeed, the kingdom of man, given him for further transformation, the kingdom of solidary freedom and cooperative production. Every branch of knowledge of the world, every new understanding through appropriate techniques of the actual state of the world, is therefore an opportunity for man's freedom and creativity. The role of the sciences, then, is the liberation of man and social advancement. It will be helpful perhaps to dwell a little on this role.

A first consideration is the fact that today there is no science which is not social *per se,* and the term "social" here has a much deeper significance than that ordinarily given it. It does not mean simply a greater interdependence between the scientific and technological approach and the socioeconomic structure, a broader presence in the fields which the total culture reserves for its institutions as well as within the separate institutions. It means, above all, that all scientific progress becomes automatically and for everyone a process of "hominization," as expressed by Chardin. This is amply demonstrated by the positions taken and the role played by outstanding contemporary scientists and the great importance which scientific research is acquiring in national budgets. There is a social awareness of the role of science which is much more profound and much broader than that sought for it by the nineteenth-century positivists. Even the disciplines which studied man's life relationships or tried to define the laws of social statics and dynamics did not have the impact or the role which contemporary society assigns to each single branch of science. Neither the "social question" nor "social problems" entered into the strictly scientific considerations of a Durkheim or a Weber, both typical of the disciplines which concentrated on the social factors of development, and so they were left to the agitators and utopians.

Although it is true that sociology has recently extended its concern to the group dimensions of scientific awareness, it is still astonishing that for the past half century it failed to grasp, in the problematic character of community living and the conspicuous conflicts of human groups, the true specific object of its study. Only within the last few years has there been mention of a sociology of peace or of war, a sociology of science. Since it is increasingly clear that the problem of social relations is one of justice in a society formerly based on labor, but now centered on leisure, science has become one of the keystones of that justice. This consists fundamentally in giving each individual greater scope for his freedom and responsibility, restoring, in other words, his place in the kingdom of the cosmos which is moving toward greater plasticity through man's action and creativeness.

The diffusion of this collective, scientific awareness is another extremely interesting element. The basic characteristic of the phenomenon of socialization, understood as a universal fact of contemporary society, is the presence of and the broad field covered by technology, which is directly dependent on scientific progress. With all its ideological and empirical implications, technology can no longer be viewed as an element introduced, or introducible, and acting in society as a datum with unforeseeable consequences. Technology today is a genuine system of social customs which assumes new types of knowledge and accelerates their attainment and which contributes to a different awareness of man's power in association with others, whether in interpersonal relationships or in his relations with nature. This fact has slowly modified and continues to modify the understanding of individual and group roles. Along with the parallel development of more efficient and self-motivating socioeconomic structures, especially in certain areas of the world, it influences the contemporary mind away from fatalistic assent to an external or superior collective spirit, which was ill defined in any case, and toward an awareness of group responsibilities. The organizing spirit characteristic of and accentuated by technique socializes almost all formerly individual activities and responsibilities and stimulates them to greater efficiency. As a result, the whole of society increasingly assumes the characteristics of a human creation, and its life increasingly takes on a consciousness and rationality that fashions itself through the goals it chooses and the plans it ordains to reach them.

In this process each science is a social possession which serves everyone and promotes progress for everyone, a kind of collective demiurgic power which can plan and organize the pursuit of its own earthly destiny. Modern scientists, therefore, are again brutally confronted with the ethical problem; being directly responsible for group destinies, they cannot evade the obligation to give their research and their work a specific direction and purpose.

The body of technical science burdens and threatens us because we are trying to employ the body without the spirit; we are trying to buy the corpse of science. We are hagridden by the power of nature which we should command, because we think its command needs less devotion and understanding than its discovery. And because we know how gunpowder works, we sigh for the days before atomic bombs. But massacre is not prevented by sticking to gunpowder; the Thirty Years' War is proof of that. Massacre is prevented by the scientist's ethic, and the poet's, and every creator's: that the end for which we work exists and is judged only by the means which we use to reach it. This is the human sum of the values of science. It is the basis of a society which scrupulously seeks knowledge to match and govern its power. But it is not the scientist who can govern society; his duty is to teach it the implications and the values in his work. . . .[12]

This vivid presentation of the scientist's role in modern society, when there is increasing awareness of the unity of nature and of mankind, leads directly to further consideration of the nature of the change in the Church. The world's progressive self-awareness is, I believe, reflected to the greatest extent in the social teaching of the Church, that is, in the field in which the principles of Christian morality are applied to human actions as being socially interrelated. Stress has been laid on the historical aspects of the Church's social teaching, and it has been accused as well of a kind of Machiavellianism, as if it had adapted to changing situations for no other reason than to safeguard its privileges. The social order depicted in its social teaching is often identified with some existing order or one which existed in the past and was considered ideal. The positive material which abounds in the social encyclicals, we must admit, was filtered from a specific culture and from historical experiences limited to a particular area of the world. This explains why these same encyclicals, although they had a worldwide audience and brought the Church out of the ghetto, have not found immediate application. It has also been said, to paraphrase the terms a little, that they were encyclicals *about* the workers, not encyclicals *addressed to* the workers.

The "social question," as such, was set within the framework of a specific system, capitalism; and it is precisely this which permitted its explosion. The initial moral—and, in certain respects, moralistic—reaction of the Church was a condemnation of the system, together with a rejection of the collectivist alternative. In practice, the Church's social teaching became a social morality used to correct the system in the firm conviction that there were not, and for the good of humanity there could not be, any valid alternatives. Finally, the social question became one of class relationships, which were to be reviewed, reformed, and healed. The still more fundamental problems which this question implied were not dealt with as preliminary matters to be solved.

In the post-World War II period, however, the Church's social teaching accepts a multiplicity of economic and social systems, in and through which the same moral norms take on different expression and importance. This is not relativism, but a recognition that the norms concern the human world in its global dimensions. The mention of different systems, ideologies, and movements in different stages of development and ethical situations is characteristic of *Mater et Magistra* and *Pacem in Terris*. These documents deal, for the first time, directly with the problem of human community, as a unity, on the basis of the imperatives deriving from human nature itself, recognizing at the same time man's autonomous effort to proclaim his rights and to define his duties at the world level. What is stressed is not so much the extent and seriousness of the problem as the global implications of every social movement or upheaval and the related role the Church assumes in its appeal to the conscience of man, as an individual and in community.

This changed perspective in the Church's social teaching immediately gave rise to the impression that her relation to the political struggle in certain areas and structures was not a close one or, in fact, did not exist at all. And it is not without reason that these recent documents and appeals are addressed to all men of good will. This very "expansion" demonstrates that the Church can change as a cultural system, and the documents themselves are a clear and precise expression of this fact.

In *Mater et Magistra* and *Pacem in Terris* the following can clearly be noted: (a) the degree of knowledge of the objective situation to which the social teaching of the Church is addressed; (b) the degree of awareness of the transformation and evolution of social needs, economic systems, and political communities; (c) the degree of knowledge of the "new" elements which are altering the social field and its dimensions; (d) the response to the increasingly clear religious imperative and to the need of a hierarchy of values; (e) the response to the need of a modern Christian spirituality and concept of the temporal world, and of commitment to it. Since it is the application of social morality—or, as Villain said, "the projection on the social plane of Christian dogma and morality"—the Church's social teaching has, of necessity, adapted to changed historical situations.

This process of adjustment—as in the case of all knowledge in the Church—proceeds, on the one hand, along the lines of development characteristic of dogma and morality, which the mind of Christ, imparted to the Church, progressively unfolds in time in a perennial pentecost of the Spirit, the true mover of the development of dogma. On the other hand, it is a response to the evolution of Christian consciousness, confronted with new and recurrent problems as situations and events demand the certainty of its faithfulness and its fidelity to reality.

In the broadest range of collective world consciousness, this means that the Church knows it cannot be identified with a particular society or culture and that it is the guarantor of values which, although they find concrete expression on the historical level, cannot be integrally and definitively translated into specific socioeconomic systems or particular political communities, because their source and final end is God. The very moment the Church "defined" a social doctrine, it would be caught in the vise of history which traps all civilizations and makes them mortal. The moment it failed to take account of the "new," it would fail in its essential mission as the extension in time of the Incarnation. It is within this framework that the "social question" has taken on a new dimension in papal documents. With the passing of the traditional quarrels between workers and employers, between public and private initiative, the social question now involves all men as members of the single, broader community of all peoples, with their most profound resources of intelligence, activity, and sacrifice. The social question means the general orientation of the life of the human community, and the Church's intervention involves a critical judgment on that orientation and on the priorities and choices it determines.

The criticism of the liberal theory, which some interpreted as a reaction to the wrongs done by liberalism to the Church, has been reinforced by the action of factors intrinsic to the mechanism of production and by today's increasingly compelling need for planning. If an economic system based entirely on the laws of supply and demand faces a crisis caused by the development of its own mechanisms and by the new theory of development, a new task devolves upon the State and the economic and social engineers, a task that postulates a higher degree of knowledge and responsibility and more immediate and more serious ethical consequences. In this sense as well, the Church's social teaching cannot be confined to class struggle or to the nth attempt to construct an ideal system in contrast to the more or less evident disorder of society. This teaching is a recall to urgent existential reality, a recall to historic expediency—if that is not too ambiguous a word—which a wise statesman must accept if he is to realize his plan. The demands of justice in the developing countries fall within this framework.

The appeal to all resources and energies, the assistance of

experts and volunteers—this is the different response, but in a sense the perennial and true-to-itself response, which the changing Church gives a changing world on the plane of knowledge.

There is no need to dwell further on the change in the Church as a cultural system because of the progressive knowledge the world is acquiring of itself. The immense range of human endeavor is too closely linked to ethical ends and to the problems of the human community, with all the various degrees of tension and accommodation motivated by moral considerations. This exposition may have served to underline, and perhaps has made a little more understandable, the type of change that is taking place, namely, one which preserves the unchangeable permanency of the principles and, at the same time, permits the unavoidable adaptation to human contingencies.

Notes

[1] C. S. Hall and G. Lindzey, *Theories of Personality* (New York, Wiley, 1957), p. 534.

[2] G. W. Allport, *Personality: A Psychological Interpretation* (New York, Holt, 1937), p. 48.

[3] *L'Evoluzione del Comportamento in un Processo di Sviluppo* (Rome, 1962), pp. 11–12.

[4] M. D. Chenu, *La Foi dans l'Intelligence,* p. 65.

[5] E. Pin, *Elementos Para una Sociologiá del Catolicismo Latino-Americano* (Fribourg-Bogota, 1963), p. 49.

[6] R. N. Bellah, "Religious Evolution," in *American Sociological Review,* Vol. 29, No. 3 (June 1964), p. 358.

[7] *Ibid.,* pp. 360–361.

[8] M. D. Chenu, *L'Evangile dans le Temps* (Paris, 1964), pp. 251–252.

[9] *Ibid.,* pp. 468–469. Cf. C. Davis, *God's Grace in History* (New York, Sheed & Ward, 1967).

[10] J. Bronowski, *Science and Human Values,* rev. ed. (New York, Harper, 1965), pp. 44–45. Reprinted by permission of Julian Messner, Division of Simon & Schuster, Inc. Copyright © 1956, by J. Bronowski.

[11] Chenu, *La Foi dans l'Intelligence,* p. 252.

[12] Bronowski, *op. cit.,* pp. 70–71.

THREE

The Church as a Social Organism

CHANGE IN THE CHURCH, viewed as a cultural system, may seem difficult, given the difficulties inherent in the evolution of dogma and of the knowledge of religious experience. Change in the Church as a social system, however, should arouse less apprehension or opposition. Sociology, it is true, has not yet succeeded in establishing a valid theoretical framework for the analysis of social change, and attempts to use functional analysis have not yielded conclusive results. Consequently, we would not—and could not—use this approach, especially since any discussion of change in a social system is, in the last analysis, a discussion of values. This part of our discussion, therefore, will be limited to some definitions of method, while those functions will be treated at greater length which every social system must fulfill if it is to subsist, have vitality, achieve integration and develop—functions which can also be applied to the Church as a religious system.

In the first place, we must avoid the temptation of thinking that social values—namely, the criteria according to which a human group judges the individual and society, organizes its collective life, develops and defines its institutions, and regulates social relationships—derive essentially from a particular teaching, and that individual decisions are so autonomous that they can be changed by individual exhortations. A value is a more or less implicit objective which is not directly questioned. For example, in a society like ours, progress in raising the living standard is a value. In sociology, a value is not characterized by a moral judgment. It is an objective which is pursued and which always has emotional overtones. Value must not be confused with "social norm," which is the means for achieving a value. A norm may evolve very rapidly depending on its effectiveness, and its rationale is therefore much more marked. Economic planning may be accepted or rejected as a means of raising living levels, according to whether or not it is considered effective. In our world there is likely to be stronger and more widespread agreement on values than on norms.

The question then arises as to how a norm can lead to the attainment of existing, but not conscious, values. This can happen because effectiveness is a value in itself, in the sense that a greater value is attributed to the means-end relationship than to the definition or acceptance of the end itself. In a given society, therefore, agreement may be reached on the norms simply because they are effective and without reference to the values; on the other hand, there may be agreement on the values simply because they are traditional, even though unrelated to or even in conflict with existing norms.

There is a very important distinction between professed values and real values. An intellectualist concept of man runs the risk of forgetting this fundamental point. Professed values can be fine, altruistic ideals which, using the criteria of "good," provide justifications for conduct and maintain so-called group morals. They may, however, without our being aware of it, fail to correspond to the real values which actually determine our conduct. In a changing world, professed values evolve more slowly than real values. For example, we defend the traditional concept of the family, but we act quite differently. This is the phenomenon known as the "cultural lag." We must be conscious of the real, concrete values which govern or ought to govern the adaptation of behavior to social life.

This consciousness can be the object of sociological study, and it can constitute the prophetic role of an institution or an individual, either in creating awareness of the changes taking place or in giving them a better long-term orientation. It is important to stress here that this prophetic role could be an activity of the Church, as already noted in the first chapter. An institution, however, cannot exercise this role unless it is sensitive to new values and understands how they emerge from factual situations.

It is also important to note that values acquire their ultimate validation, not from the efficacy of the norms for attaining them, but from their organic relationship to human life and to each other, from the dynamic day-to-day understanding of them in the group consciousness. Too often a great deal of time is wasted discussing norms without interpreting the "reality" of the social values. Rather than studying opinions—

which reflect professed values—it is preferable to seek out the real values which actually govern behavior. For this reason, it is neither useful nor necessary in the present analysis to proceed deductively from principles or from the theological definition of the nature of the Church. We must begin with the facts undeniably related to the social environment in which the life of the world and of the Church are developing and which is characterized by a number of unquestioned elements: the increasing importance of technology, economic expansion, transition from a civilization based on labor to one centered on leisure, etc. These facts are of a structural order in society, and they are important from the viewpoint of this analysis precisely to the degree in which they pose urgent new problems for mankind. The solutions sought and adopted for these problems produce reactions and common modes of behavior which give rise to new views on life. As a result, many presentations of the Christian message, many pastoral customs and attitudes toward membership in the religious group, become outmoded. Just as new forms of awareness are necessary to bring to maturity the change in the Church as a cultural system, so, in the evolutionary process now going on, there is need of basic actions and clear-cut decisions capable of restoring the effectiveness of real values in social thought, along with new norms whose justification will be the result of enlightened action rather than merely the influence of tradition.

With these premises, we may proceed to a consideration of the functions of the Church as a social system, using a general outline quite commonly followed in sociology. First, however, it is necessary to make an important distinction between functions and mechanisms. P. Tufari explains this as follows:

Rather than the number and quality of means at the disposal of the system, mechanism here means the way in which these means are combined to realize a given function. It is distinct from function because, in social phenomena, there is not, as in biological phenomena, a fixed pattern or map to which reference is constantly made. The best a surgeon can do is to lead back his patient to the state of "normal," where there is no need for any other surgical intervention. But in social facts, there are no ready made models and the problem of adapting means to ends is generally left to the free play of interests, of mistakes, of successful intuitions, of good will and of the possibilities and limits of human action.

As applied to the sociology of religion this distinction is most important. It opens the way for further comparisons between one religious system and another. Comparison can be made at three levels: 1. Do there exist functions which all religious systems consider as essential for their existence as religious systems? 2. Do there exist functions which are considered as essential by some and as non-essential by others? 3. Which are the mechanisms which a given system uses to ensure a given function?

The problem of mediation between man and the divinity (communication, interpretation of the divine will, presence of God to man, and presence of man to God) may serve as an example of a constantly recurring problem which has received different solutions in the various systems.

The way is also clear for the fuller understanding of the internal problems of a given system. With the passing of time there can be a danger of identifying function and mechanism, i.e., the thing to get and the way one seeks to get it.

In any case, the natural result of this ambiguity appears to be a logical refusal to think intelligently. The words "it has always been so" may indicate either the self-assurance of those who never doubt that this is "the way to act" or the skeptical resignation of those who see that there is nothing they can do about it: or it can even indicate the impending destruction of the system because of the failure to recognize that, while the mechanism must be changed, this change has to be carried out in such a way that the function is not only left intact, but realized better.

For those who are interested both in the doctrinal understanding and in the problems of action in a given religious system, the meaning of this distinction between function and mechanism is clear. Here it must be pointed out that the particular contribution of functional analysis, rather than the discovery of this distinction, is its attempt to render it "practical"—as far, of course, as empirical observation is possible in such a dangerous field. On the one hand, the validity of a given mechanism can be tested by taking into account the function it is meant to perform and on the other hand the importance of a function can be adequately checked only by examining the activity, modification or suppression of given mechanisms. . . .[1]

The permanent relationship between functions and mechanisms in the Church must be analyzed in detail, since the latent functions in this type of community are more vital than in other systems and the mechanisms used are justified in a different manner. For example, the emergence of a popular religious movement is much more unpredictable, and its consequences much more uncontrollable, than the action of a political party, because of the undercurrent of motivations and stimuli whose nature and influence cannot be classified in rational categories and which are not openly professed in social behavior. The same may be said of mechanisms. To what extent, for example, can the use of material means to spread the message and worship be justified by clear theological proofs or be easily ascribed, instead, to a hidden simony.

FUNCTION AND MECHANISM OF CONSERVATION

The structure of the system must be preserved in essential lines. The means which assure the permanency of beliefs, rites, traditions, norms and institutions within the community, must exist in such a way that, with the passing of time, with changing situations with the coming of the different generations, the religious system may retain its characteristics and its capacity to "interest" the individual and communal life of its members.[2]

This fundamental function gives rise, logically, to definite mechanisms and creates a particular mentality. In the Church the concept of "tradition" assumes several meanings which are not always distinguishable because of the complexity which surrounds them and the ambiguities they conceal. First of all, the concept is bound up with the historical origins of the religion, but not as in every historical religion which is accompanied by a "tradition." Together with the fundamental beliefs and values which form the basis of the "social memory" of the group, there is in the Church the responsible conserving action through a social organ, the magisterium. In the second place, from a more historicist viewpoint, the concept of tradition in the Western world has been associated in practice with a particular system of ownership and identification. The analysis of this aspect presents numerous difficulties, for it involves the very concept of law and power. Now it is well-known that, in the course of time, Canon Law underwent profound modifications, and the authority of the Church, vis-à-vis the State, was respected and recognized with reference to historical situations and the general progress of civil institutions. It cannot be denied, of course, that Canon Law codified the rights and privileges of the Church as a religious community in a preexisting order and that it also adopted the "ownership" pattern of Roman law. But it is precisely the historical antecedent that gradually produced confusion in the "internal gradations of the papal function."

Given its extreme initial usefulness in establishing solid guarantees for tradition, juridical centralization eventually tied its fate, sociologically, to the maintenance of certain structures. The changes which did take place were, in fact, internal changes within these structures, and it is only Vatican Council II which produced a crisis in the relationship once considered absolutely necessary. In actual practice, the sociological bonds between tradition and structure and the pertinent changes they underwent also permitted, for the conservation of the system, the transition from a concept of property based on land ownership to the more modern concept of negotiable capital. The mentality of conservation and defense was smartened and reinforced, whereas the Church is actually an *assembly* of the children of God who preserve the "deposit" of religion—and the material structures necessary to them as human beings—in order to offer it, to give it to all men. The function of conserving the faith was gradually transformed into conserving the mechanisms considered valid or necessary for carrying out this function, while the juridical norms became more important than the values which they were intended to conserve and to spread.

A similar transition took place in a function derived from conservation, namely, identification. It cannot be ignored that the Church as a social system, with its institutions and group activities, needs an embodiment in the temporal order. This "incorporation" takes place within broader systems (a fact clearly evident today in the minority situation in which the Church finds itself in the world) with which it must enter into contact, since the faithful live in a definite network of social relationships set within a juridical system under the social authority which represents or governs them. In order to conserve the system, material means are necessary, and their control, use, and exchange are generally the same for all according to the law of social justice. The Church was recognized as a legal person from the time of Constantine; and it repaid this recognition, especially during the dark period of the barbarian invasions, by safeguarding the law itself and by fostering a higher form of integration between the Roman and Germanic concepts of law.

Here again, it was not possible to avoid a sociological identification between a property system and the conservation function; in addition, this identification was pushed to the extent of backing claims and legal rights which the historical climate did not even question.

The conservation function of the Church, as a social system which must survive, is closely linked with its parallel in the global society. Charismatic tension has always thrust the Church, or certain groups within the Church, beyond concern for the preservation of a particular *status quo* in civil society; but institutional tension has led to the creation of inevitable sociological blocs with groups which guaranteed the recognition of its legal position. This is no reason to be scandalized, for there is no law which requires members of the Church to live without the support and protection of positive law. A purely spiritual Church is not possible because it would not be human. For its survival the Church will always have to cope with all the material means and instruments indispensable for maintaining places of worship, for administration, communication, and the like.

The headlong change taking place in recent years has, in a sense, exaggerated opposing tendencies, with the introduction of such terms as "Vatican finance" and "Church of the poor." But two elements have clearly emerged: on the one hand, a change in the concept of the right to property which, since the time of the Industrial Revolution, has been moving out of the context of land ownership; on the other, a change of perspective regarding the support and mobility of the strictly ecclesiastical personnel, which is the prime-motive force in the conservation of the system.

In the more recent papal documents and Council schemata, the right to private ownership is increasingly expressed in terms of a stewardship. Stewardship implies *use* and, therefore, carries with it a justification different from the earlier juridical formulation. In addition, the role changes, and innovations which have upset the general social structure have also caused a crisis with regard to the clergy's traditional manner of living and working in an exclusively ecclesiastical role. It has even been proposed that the priest, instead of being engaged in full-time ministry, might specialize in certain pastoral sectors and work and live on his earnings like any other human being.

Here it should be noted that the connection between benefices and ecclesiastical offices—which, as the basis of a certain institutional continuity, is for that very reason more strictly and exclusively clerical—has begun to disappear. The benefices for the most part are not land revenues, nor can they be supplemented much longer by government subsidies stipulated in concordats. The offices are not such as to require a full-time priest and, therefore, do not justify this traditional conservation effort. Here, too, confusion between function and mechanism must be avoided, in view of the fact that the function of conservation, in the modern setting, has been freed from the burdens imposed by property.

The Conciliar—and, in a broader sense, the ecclesial—debates produced a series of confrontations which the press had a fine time describing as struggles between "liberals" and "conservatives." The problem for the Church today is to keep all these within the fold but to refuse as its official representatives those who, forgetful of the nature and instrumental character of the conservation mechanisms, still use them—and insist that they continue to be used—in a context which the course of history has liquidated. It is precisely its capacity for change in this area that will be the Church's best response to its unrenounceable function to conserve the deposit of faith for all men of every time.

FUNCTION AND MECHANISM
OF INTEGRATION

Conservation is the work of all the members. But it is also the work of each according to the particular role which corresponds to his particular status. . . . In order to be able to speak of a religious "system," it is necessary to ensure the integration of the parts, the fitting in of the new members in the community, a form of co-ordination which checks disgregation, prevents and corrects rivalries, useless duplication of work, tension between private interests and the common good, and which finally assumes collaboration.[3]

The function of integration in a religious system is undoubtedly the most difficult and demanding. It relates to the psychological and sociological bases for membership in the system and requires a constant effort of adjustment between the subject and object of religious life, a true foundation of conscious belonging. Although the problem of religious adherence has only recently become the object of specific analysis, it has been advanced in urgent terms, even apart from its particular character. Social change has shuffled together all the standards of behavior of every human group. Within the more general context of the development of modern society, religioethical motivations can be analyzed as having a specific origin and influence in the total social system with its relative "zones of anomie." However, all the phenomena associated with contemporary change, while highlighting the dimensions of the crisis gripping the whole social structure, have immediate, inevitable, and decisive repercussions on religious motivations and attitudes, thereby positing the integrative function in new terms. Take, for example, the phenomena of migration and urbanization. Every type of mobility affects religious membership due to the disintegration of the primary groups, the establishment of new centers of assimilation, and the new psychological situations which arise when behavior is removed from the traditional channels of control. But this is a limited diagnosis. The Church certainly represents a system of metahistorical values which can undergo change, as noted in our first chapter. But these values may appear—and sometimes have actually been—"dysfunctional" in relation to the global society when this society is composed mainly of nonbelievers, or even of believers who, when new structures are evolving, prefer new values which question all forms of conduct and even the very need of identification in traditional terms.

It is precisely in this sense that the "cultural lag" between norms and values and between professed and real values is to be understood. Everyone deplores today the absence of the *ubi consistam,* or, in other words, the lack of integration; conflicts pushed to the extreme are but relative, temporary— although acute—expressions of this lack. In the high winds of social change, a major part is played by the interaction between social groups—especially new groups—and by the objective knowledge of technical mechanisms and of new social techniques for the exercise and control of power, along with the acknowledged and ambiguous phenomenon of "democratizing" everything. The effects of this process on the acceptance of the norms and values of the various groups, including the religious group, are unavoidable.

In phenomenological terms, it may be said that the broadening of the immediate psychological field introduces new standards and new models. Given the different types of motivation and the new climate of competition among roles, groups, and institutions (which seem to be foundering in flat relativism with no value scale), personal awareness of belonging is in a state of permanent crisis. How much more difficult it is on the religious level, therefore, to crack the narrow provincialism of local mentalities that are identified with ethnic, community, or national values and to reestablish universal ideas external to and transcending the traditional religious microstructures (parishes, secretariats of Catholic organizations, religious orders, etc.). Adjustment between the subject and object of religious life and the integration of personality are extremely difficult, and even more difficult is integration—whether formal or informal—between one group and another within the religious system. What the Council has done is to pose this problem on the world level. Now, writes Father Pin,

every human act takes place where two worlds meet, that of the acting subject and that of the objective reality. Both are composed of a sum of discontinuous determinations, each of which forms whole, concrete phenomena which are partially distinct and have different life rhythms. There are multiple opportunities for the exercise of human liberty in both the world of the subject and that of the object, and especially where the two meet in what is always partial accommodation.

. . . Subjective needs and desires are matched by objects determined by the sum of local, historical, and psychological conditions which are independent of the subject. . . . Choices, therefore, are limited and partly inadequate; but a minimum adequacy is necessary.[4]

In the relationship between subject and object, there is a broad area of sociological conditioning in which human freedom is exercised, and it should be remembered that this very relationship—under the disquieting pressures which changing social rhythms and the "collective representations" themselves produce in intellectual, emotional, and ethical relations—makes integration that much more difficult.

From a simple listing of phenomena, it is evident that the problem of integration is of fundamental importance (and no mention has been made here, except in passing, of the psychological aspects). The changes that have occurred or are currently taking place with regard to religious adherence, together with widespread neglect of the practice of religion or neglect of the observance of traditional religious customs, mean that we are faced with new typologies. These were formerly of a more sociological nature; today they are more personal and may even serve to prove the hypothesis of a linear process of transition from "indigenous" to "elective" religions. In any case, it is easy to see that the problem of ensuring the integrative function, even within the religious system alone, is posed in an entirely different manner. All the mechanisms of integration (e.g., standards for accepting new members, coordination to avoid disgregation or the dissipation of energies, organisms to guarantee unity and avoid tensions) must, therefore, be reexamined.

But it is important to note that the problems of integration must also be viewed on quite another level. The unity of Catholics, for example, too often invoked in a posture of opposition (the "necessity" to be united *against* something or other, the attitude of opposition and defensiveness characteristic of the councils which preceded Vatican II, etc.) has been gradually asserting itself as such a vigorous reality that—over and above the different schools of thought—this unity is possible only when there is a sharp distinction between the essential and the contingent. In social terms, it has refound in new ways its ancient symbol and social guarantee in the Supreme Pontiff. Now this unity is not a static feature of the Church; it is also her way of entering into dialogue. The analysis of internal changes cannot fail to facilitate integration with other churches and religious groups, especially in areas where separation and opposition are due not only to theological reasons but also to the interpretation of the integrative function—which, in practice, excluded any alternatives as well as any dialogue. The internal conflicts between norms and values freed repressed energies which, in the end, nourished the sense of unity (for they were identified with what was essential to the religious group), and they have also raised again the problem of religious integration, first on the inter-confessional and then on the world level. From a sociological viewpoint, it is clear that the change has broken organizational patterns, that mobility has produced crises in traditional groups, that socialization has recast the structure of power and of social control and has rejected concepts of natural or spontaneous socioeconomic development by accepting the trend to conscious direction of the process of social development toward fixed goals.

This macroscopic phenomenon has had an impact on ecclesiastical structures insofar as they were linked to specific areas or groups, were isolated in defensive minority ghettos or impregnable privileged majorities, or were concerned with their own preservation or that of their "patrimony" of whatever kind. In social pluralism, persons of different confessions necessarily rubbed shoulders as the specialization of social functions, their diffusion, and their control, confined entirely to the role involved, liberalized social life. Hence there arose forms of solidarity and activity inspired by human, or sometimes purely functional, values divorced from any religious inspiration and profession whatever. In this no-man's-land, awareness of a common "deposit," to be developed as well as defended, and of an integration that could be accomplished only through religious values—the only ones that do not disintegrate under the impact of affluence or the nameless terror of the atomic nightmare—has pushed Catholics, Protestants, and Orthodox toward a common center of faith and action. Spiritual riches grow in the giving; they are not dissipated. The search for what unites dissolves old divisions and deep-seated rivalries. For this broader function the Church has thought of more flexible and useful mechanisms of integration, and she must continue to do so. The urgency has been recognized, for example, in the new regulations for mixed marriages, derived from the Decree on Ecumenism; but the road ahead is a long one.

These observations lead to another series of considerations on the Church's integrative function with respect to the world, in aspects directly linked with the social structure. The sense of possessing an absolute truth cannot prevent the acceptance of the existing pluralism of different civilizations. Historically speaking, there has been too great an integration between Catholicism and the so-called West, between Catholicism and certain nations. It took the direct, eloquent—and, for the first time, universal—confrontation in the Ecumenical Council to impel the Church to lay aside her Mediterranean dress and to pay greater attention to the historical values of new and ancient cultures. This is not to say that this obligation had not been perceived for centuries at the center of Christianity, even when Church administration was most highly centralized. The Church as a social system came to maturity at the crossroads of three civilizations: Hebrew, Greek, and Roman. But integration with the whole contemporary world is just beginning and can be achieved only on the basis of recognizing the values of "the others." For this, neither a rapprochement at the summit, official directives, or knowledge derived solely from books will ever be sufficient.

No integration of any kind is possible without dialogue, and no dialogue is possible unless one accepts one's interlocutor and unless there is confidence that a more complete manifestation of the truth can result from the encounter. Although the world's march toward unity is furthered by science and technology, with the innumerable consequences these entail, it is still obstructed by the many pronounced differences in social structures and cultural systems, and it is brusquely interrupted at times by economic imbalances. The Council has clearly indicated the integrative function which the Church can exercise in today's world. It not only brought together the representatives of Catholic churches throughout the world and invited representatives of the Christian denominations to be present, but it also provided the opportunity for all the ethnic, geographical, economic, social, and cultural differences which they represented to find expression, confrontation, and unity. Within its living body the Church absorbs, purifies, and renews all that is human and mortal, even the various civilizations and systems, for they too are transitory and mortal. The Church has shown its readiness to integrate into its knowledge, symbols, cultural expressions, discipline, and style the whole spontaneous ferment bubbling and rising throughout mankind. It is not within our competence to list the appropriate institutions, means, and methods for the exercise of this function; and it is, in any case, extremely difficult to define them since they are in the same process of evolution

as the world in which we live. It is possible only to note that
the Church's integrative function is very different from that
ascribed to it by the exponents of the organicist view, and it
cannot be fulfilled unless secularization and theocracy are
abandoned. Within the diminishing space created by progress,
the world accepts—and, indeed, expects—a call to unity; but it
tolerates no ambiguities, nor can it await any longer the definition of concepts and the end of nominalist disputes.

It is within this context that the Church's present integrative
mechanisms—certain aspects of which are already undergoing
profound modifications—are to be analyzed. I believe that the
changes—when, where, and to the extent that they take place
—are being determined by certain basic principles.

In the first place, a process of revision, in some ways unconscious and therefore creating a kind of bewilderment, has been
going on in all those temporal activities of the Church which
are rooted in particular historic situations or social structures
and which, throughout almost all the world, hinder integration
with the living values of the country in which they are taking
place. The process of decolonization, the emergence of new
nations and new types of culture and societal structures, exact
a tremendous effort of purification and clarification. They also
demand a calculated risk which only faith can make accepta-
ble. We are at a turning point. A number of bishops have
already rounded that turn and have indicated their method of
doing so, which requires further verification. But it must also
be admitted that there are countercurrents which militate
against the integration of the Church with the world and

which create divisions that are more than ideological within the Catholic group.

In the second place, and as a consequence of the foregoing, a choice must be made once and for all between the spiritual efficacy and the social efficacy of the Church's activities, for it must cease to be identified in its first approach—or even, as some think, in its reason for being—as a social institution. The growing phenomenon of secularization, already discussed on the cultural level, raises alternatives which have direct sociopolitical repercussions unless the Church reverts to what it is essentially: a religious institution. Similarly, and for the same reasons, a choice must also be made between spiritual efficacy and economic efficiency in the matter of integrative mechanisms, for such a great expenditure of energies cannot and must not be governed by the profit motive.

How many times has the Church become integrated into a particular area or group with no lively concern for the universal dimension of the religious role and has been dragged along by social success and economic yield in its choice of integrative tools. The first consequence of the revision of institutions and activities, which is already going on in certain areas, will be reflected in the selection and training of personnel—and this is also already happening. The formation of the Christian and of the priest must be set in a different framework, and methods must be found to guarantee its continuation so that the Church's personnel will not again contribute to the delays in integration which outdated mechanisms created for it. In this sense, care must be taken that the primary

integration—that within the Church—is really closely related
to its external integration, which is the more urgent with respect to the world.

FUNCTION AND MECHANISM
OF ADAPTATION

Conservation and integration do not happen in a vacuum. There
is a constant reference to the "outside world" to which life must
be constantly adjusted. A religious system, in a process analogous
to that of an organism submitted to changes in temperature, excess
of exertion and environmental difficulties, is constantly under fire
from ideas, groups, institutions and events which, from outside,
tend to penetrate the structure of the system. A religious system
which is unable to adjust itself continuously to new situations without losing its essential characteristics is a system which is destined
to perish like any other organism which has lost its ability to
adapt itself to its environment.[5]

   This basic function requires interpretation and evaluation of
the different tendencies both within a social system and external to it, and then a true and proper adaptation. Scholars
have tried to define more or less precisely the normal tendencies of social action in order to understand their motivation, to
determine to what degree they are manifest or latent, and to
deduce the extent of their influence on behavior (conformist,
deviant, etc.).
   To exercise its adaptive function, a social system must know
and acknowledge the "signs of the times" to which the perti-

nent mechanisms should be adjusted. In contemporary sociology, functional analysis applied to the external tensions which give rise to defensive reaction is among the most useful approaches in analyzing social change. In fact, the application of this type of analysis to the action of the Church has been one of the most valid proofs of the theory's usefulness. J. M. G. Thurlings, in an essay entitled "Functionalism, Social Change and the Sociology of Religion,"[6] analyzes the social change that has occurred in the Church together with the consequent progressive indifference of the faithful. He argues that this indifference came about because of the presence and activity of secular institutions, which appeared as functional alternatives to the ecclesiastical institution. The latter was going beyond its primary—or religious—sphere of competence and assuming "compensatory" tasks (organizing social groupings and institutions based on religious affiliation, such as schools, hospitals, youth movements, trade unions, etc.). And he ascribes the indifference also to the weakening of the ecclesiastical control mechanism. It is a question of those currents of energy or knowledge—to use Parsons' phrase[7]—which penetrate the social and cultural system (at all levels: the individual, the group, the global society) and which destroy its equilibrium by introducing new areas of power and new privileges. The Church, Thurlings rightly maintains, defended itself as a social system against this double threat to its existence by a corresponding readaptation, creating new mechanisms and strengthening others. The Church has, in fact, concentrated its activity in certain fields in order to increase its influence in the external world; it has isolated and barricaded itself within particular areas and specific sectors, actually aided by the external attack which sharpens the sense of belonging. And the Church has changed its internal structure by revising the respective roles and competencies of the clergy and the laity.

In a certain historic framework, it can be seen to what extent the Church's social teaching and its doctrine on relations with civil power was able to change precisely because of the situation outlined above. It can also be observed how isolation, on the one hand, and the efforts toward unity and internal cohesion, on the other, have contributed to a series of more creative positions with respect to the non-Christian world. In any case, the Council has clearly shown that the Church can change through this adaptive function by choosing *aggiornamento* as its most direct goal. This involves revision of the system of knowledge of both the ecclesiastical and the external worlds, revision of the communication system within the ecclesiastical world and between it and the external world, and revision of the social control within the ecclesiastical world and of its comportment toward the external world. It is clear that this function—in direct contact with the living needs which arise or are introduced in the Church (without waiting for bureaucracy to shift its slow and sticky gears)—is essential to the Church, and it is equally clear that the mechanisms of adaptation must be changed with greater speed and flexibility.

In today's world, research on social facts, fundamental perspectives of various human groups, and public opinion must be recognized as normal channels of information. This has happened in the Church, under the pressure of events, but there should be official awareness and recognition of their importance and necessity. The preparatory work for the Council revealed the slowness and inadequacy of the Curial mechanisms for adaptation. Only the Conciliar debates, thanks to the free and open climate introduced by Pope John's opening address, were able later and with deplorable loss of time to accomplish what should have been done by the organisms assigned to the preparatory investigative task. Pius XII had called for the formation of public opinion in the Church in 1956, but it was the Council which demonstrated its importance and, in so doing, also demonstrated how the Church changes.

It must also be pointed out that the techniques of communication cannot be adopted merely as instruments. With respect to its use of the tools of communication, the Church merits no reproach. Radio, television and a specialized press have been part of the ecclesiastical mechanisms of adaptation for many years. The use of these media was, in fact, promoted and given considerable relevance by the fact that the Vatican is also a State, with services similar to those of other States. What has become increasingly clear only recently is the value of social communication in itself as an opportunity for dialogue with and presence in the world. In addition, there remains the problem of improving the selection and training of personnel for the adaptive mechanisms, along with that of creating new systems of communication between Church and State. The Council debate on this point focussed sharp attention on the Vatican's diplomatic service and the training of the personnel assigned to it. The social significance of diplomatic representation in the Church, insofar as there is a Vatican City

State, was questioned, and it was charged that local situations were not adequately or fully represented at the center of Christianity. Unless broader channels are opened up for the flow of information and for special missions carried out by expert personnel, the process of adaptation is bound to fail. In a dynamic world it is not enough to have organisms for representation; opinions and experiences, which go far beyond the traditional type of diplomatic representation, must be interpreted and coordinated by competent personnel. Even in a period of transition, although possible and necessary to use the personnel available, training is needed over and above the career apprenticeships in nunciature secretariats. In any case, the interpenetration between the local sociocultural traditions and the living organism of the Church goes far beyond the issue of diplomatic representation.

The permanent function of the Council in the ecclesiastical structure is, I think, to be analyzed along the same lines. The calling of Vatican II was undoubtedly motivated by an anxious desire for adaptation which was already present at all levels within the Church. The problem now is to translate this function, which was so well perceived and carried out in the concentrated period of the Council, into a mechanism or series of mechanisms in which none of the vitality aroused within the Church and in its relations with the world will be lost. Because what the Council proposes is a conscious revision of the Church's action in the world in view of the changes in the world and in the development of Catholic theology, the Council calls for a new formula and more agile mechanism. To refuse to update the mechanism would—in this case more than in any other perhaps—mean a refusal to revise the Church as a social system and, therefore, would frustrate the intentions and decisions of the Council. The proposal of the Council Fathers—which Pope Paul VI accepted and made his own— to establish a senate of bishops, easy to consult and permitting of quick consideration and wise and timely decisions, is one of the measures which is most responsive to the exigencies that emerged in the Council and which assures it a kind of permanent function in the modern Church. The idea of more frequent councils that would concentrate on specific subjects and issues is within this same line of thinking.

It is basically the Church's *action* which requires continuous adaptation, and apart from appropriate integrations and the development of theological thought, it is the now irreversibly "pastoral" nature of the Council which needs continuing mechanisms, for these are the means through which the action of the Church becomes evident. If once the phrase was *Ecclesia semper reformanda,* we may now rightly affirm, in the proper context, *mechanismi* (read Curia) *semper reformandi.* The senate of bishops will also need instrumentalities other than the traditional ones. And it is already clear that, alongside the Roman bureaucrats (in fact no longer Roman now, but from the whole world), the Church will have to establish, in an official and responsible manner, essential functions for the whole range of "experts" whom it called together for the Council. New statuses, new roles, and pertinent controls will have to be defined. At its present speed, however, history will not pause for the formulation of rules and criteria in order to give a little breathing space. The process of adaptation, therefore, will have to be experimental and controlled. There are already some "directorships" whose final form cannot yet be fixed, but whose flexibility allows for the use of all energies.

The Conciliar commissions, which are obviously needed to transfer the Council decisions to the living ecclesial body, must also have the most supple mechanisms at their disposal for another fundamental reason: the Council has set in motion many charisms; the Church is permeated with them and, as in other epochs, is itself passing through a charismatic period. The accelerated history we live today does not permit the transition from charismatic moment to institutional renewal to move as it did after the Council of Trent or even after Vatican I.

FUNCTION AND MECHANISM
OF DEVELOPMENT

Integration and adjustment are processes which are instrumental for the developing conservation of the organism. Development depends on the characteristics and aims of the system and may mean the constantly growing, conscious and active sharing of the members in the life of the system or the growth of institutions or the increase of the numbers of the faithful through missionary work or self-affirmation in terms of prestige, recognition and competition. In more general terms, it means the function which assures a religious system of approaching dynamically towards its ultimate goal, i.e., the accomplishment of the "mission" to which it is destined.[8]

The function of development requires a long-range view which clearly distinguishes the provisional from the essential, which places its emphasis on the most suitable choices of time, place, methods of action, and plans for the future disposition of personnel and resources.

Christian eschatology exerts enormous influence on the view taken of the Church's future on the historic level, just as it influences the formulation of the theology of history and earthly realities. The perspective of religious action is, in fact, always metahistorical, and the tension between incarnation and eschatology is permanent in the Christian's life and action. The debate on whether or not a philosophy of history that is not also a theology of history is possible, however, is unquestionably due to the monastic stress on a Western stream of theological thought and to the revival of the sacred as a social institution (and, therefore, to the distinction between sacred and secular which intruded on the other distinction between holy and pagan). There was projected into the Church the drama of a priestly class which was obliged to live in the world and which—by definition—did not act in this world nor with the things of this world but on all Christianity. The Letter to Diognetus seems to have been written yesterday, until we remember that for several centuries it was stuck in a theological parenthesis due to the development of a monastic ideal which was applied to all the faithful in an increasingly individualistic and ideal framework and which shut the Christian up in a tower for protection and defense. This mental complex, in effect, debilitated the characteristics of renewal and com-

munity proper to Christian action and blocked the development of the Church. No missionary effort today can be based
on the idea of saving one's own soul, and no modern man
justifies any social action, direct or indirect, on the grounds
that his aim is to save his own soul.

Without going more deeply into these observations, we must
emphasize the extent to which this mental complex exerts a
determining influence on the view taken of the Church's development as a social organism, on the attitude toward the social authority and commitment of its members, and, finally,
on the method of establishing a scale of priorities in decisions
of a general nature. The most obvious tension in this influence
is that between the elite and the masses. Consideration of the
function of development, and consequently the arrangement
of mechanisms, will differ depending on whether we start
from the fact of being a majority or minority group and, also,
whether we think only in terms of long-range expectations
across the vast checkerboard of the world. It is undeniable that
a Catholicism which, according to optimistic projections, will
comprise only 8 or 9 percent of the total world population by
the year 2000 will adopt measures quite different from those
based on the assumption of an all-embracing triumphalism at
every level. It is likewise undeniable that the formulation of
the problem of development in realistic terms has an enormous
impact on the motives for belonging to the religious group, on
the structure of the dialogue with other religions, and on the
way in which the prestige of the religious group is conceived
in relation to other religions and to the world. The important
thing is to face the subject squarely and to extract from it,

without prejudice to the final outcome, the outline of a "policy" on the basis of the signs of the times, which are the reminders of Providence in history.

In any event, the developing function requires a general view of the ministry of the Church, of the different historic methods used by the institutions created for its exercise, and, finally, of the available structures for promotion. This broad overview—which must stem from a central point of reference, like a sensitive antenna with a global range—permits the re-evaluation of every local detail and every regional or sectoral difference within the broader perspective, providing the basis for a consequent distribution of forces and coordination at every level to guarantee the maximum efficiency that can be humanly expected of them.

No one denies this broad general vision; in fact, everyone affirms it. There is the danger, however, that it may evanesce in some mediatory arrangement or in a simple recognition of the diversity in unity. For effective development action, it is indispensable to adopt a positive outlook and a uniform methodology, subject to conscientious review in planning and directing activity. It is not surprising—especially if we consider postwar pastoral activity—that projections of the Church's action must necessarily be based on positive data and scientific methods, even though the central frame of reference must remain the theological background. Too often a blind trust in Providence, on which we unload our own inertia, and the promise of the Church's indefectibility, which gives rise to authoritarianism and presumption, make us slow to use the irreplaceable contribution of experiential and positive knowledge or, even, cause us to deny the dialectic value of doubt and correction in what concerns the Church's action. The salvation of souls—to use the theological term—cannot be postponed at will, nor can it dispense us from fulfilling the salvific mission which is mindful of the parable of the sheep and the goats. We have already witnessed in the Church a progressive awareness of the developing function which has come to maturity through an adaptation to the spirit of the times, the foresight of several leaders, and the courage of a number of pioneers. Today it has become a collective awareness which is an integral part of being Christian. This is what is meant by the phrase that the Christian is essentially a missionary.

The establishment of the Congregation of the Propagation of the Faith was one of the most intelligent undertakings in the history of the Church from the viewpoint of development, for among other things it maintained and enriched the religious motivation which produced it. This historical success took Catholicism permanently out of its Mediterranean framework and, as a consequence, although only after three centuries, furnished the point of departure for the Ecumenical Council. But missionary activity must be modernized and its methods made dynamic through forms of aid and services which will be more effective in ensuring the process of evangelization. It is precisely in this frontier Congregation, which is perhaps the most typical for analysis of the developing function, that the most interesting questions have arisen and will continue to arise for the whole People of God. Some aspects of the Church's social activity have been challenged, or are in a state of crisis, due to the recent emergence of newly independent countries. At the same time, a number of highly valid experiments have been carried out with a flexible approach and a kind of institutional fluidity. As a result, the Propagation of the Faith, with respect to the developing function it must ensure, is also the Congregation which is most alive and, in a certain sense, the most open to renewal. But, like other mechanisms, it also runs the risk of being behindhand, since the changes with which it must keep pace are occurring so fast and are completely new in many respects, even for the traditional experts in this field.

The example of this Congregation is the most evident, but these comments are valid for the whole system of mechanisms utilized to ensure the full exercise of the various functions. They are valid for the developing function from another viewpoint, namely, the inescapable need for coordinating financial resources and the distribution of funds and subsidies with pastoral plans for development. There is an old tendency for whole dioceses to make long-term plans on the basis of available or projected finances. In view of this and in relation to the developing function, the problem of programming economic activity as the indispensable support of pastoral action must be faced. I am not afraid of exposing myself to criticism if I say that the Church's financial system needs no revision or modernization to improve its presence in the market, but that what it does need is further theological-juridical justifications if its legitimacy in a social body that defines itself as transcendent by vocation is to be based on solid arguments. To be effective in the function of development, the Church's financial system must be clearly directed to a religious purpose and more closely related to pastoral plans than to investment earnings. Development, even when animated by the holiest of intentions, must necessarily find its wherewithal in the economic field. It must be pursued, however, so as to be clearly guaranteed a support that is as necessary as it is instrumental, and not to provide a religious cover for undertakings governed or prompted by the profit motive.

This aspect of development is too closely associated with that of the "Church of the poor," and its consequences for the promotional activity which the Church desires or ought to carry out are too evident, to require further elaboration. Just as the Church's sources of income changed in the course of time from land revenue to investments, so too changes must occur in a more rational use of voluntary contributions, longer-range planning for the undertakings guaranteed by experts, and, above all, a set of clear priorities determined by pastoral needs and urgencies. Some inequalities in the distribution of financial aid will disappear—and many have already disappeared precisely because the Council brought several requirements into proper focus—with the growing conviction that a businesslike approach and method, together with a climate of greater courage and responsibility, must be unreservedly introduced in this whole area. So long as anonymity is maintained, it will be necessary to pay much more for simple equipment than it should cost—as happened with needless expenditures for the Council, simply because the plans were based on what I would call the theological calculations of those who wanted it to end in two or three months.

The function of development also requires a sound personnel

policy. This is a complex matter rendered all the more difficult by the fact that it is impossible to speak of personnel, especially in terms of directors and leaders, in a social system like the Church without encountering or colliding with its sacral aspects. A discussion of this is better handled by those who have already gone into some of its specifics, and I shall confine these remarks, therefore, to some of the progress already made to show that possibilities for change exist.

The first type of training the Church undertook from the fourth century onward, when the spread of Christianity beyond the urban centers posed the problem of the direction of Christian communities being established in "pagan" surroundings, was primarily unitary. A strict relationship, not justified theologically but prompted by the circumstances, was reestablished between the Catholic priesthood and the old Levitical system: this meant the appointment of persons chosen for that purpose (*cleros*) to the office of minister for life, with a role fixed and distinct from any other social status.

The second type—with consequences for all Christianity— emerged from the Council of Trent, which established seminaries with a special discipline and well-defined curricula. On the basis of this training structure, which was imitated, adopted, and amplified by many religious congregations, the Church strengthened its action in recent centuries and suffered no severe shock or loss except at the beginning of the Industrial Revolution when the changes were so great and so swift that the consequences for the professions and their vocational aspects were inescapable. Today, perhaps for the first time in its history, the Church is confronted with a serious lack of per-

sonnel, precisely at a time when it has the greatest need and
when both new types of specialization and the revision of
pastoral and missionary activities are being proposed. The
tasks entrusted to the laity, in unacknowledged revival of their
origins, do not eliminate but rather aggravate the problem of
strictly ecclesiastical personnel, for, among other reasons, they
refute in many ways the traditional view of the Church as a
divine undertaking carried on solely by churchmen rather than
by the whole People of God.

It is impossible to discuss the function of development without a radical consideration of this problem. Roles, functions,
spheres of activity, and competencies and responsibilities of the
clergy must be clearly defined. More adequate mechanisms of
formation are needed, and greater attention must be paid to
psychological and sociological criteria in recruitment and selection. The more urgent needs cannot permit the waste of available energies in ineffective and sterile channels. Planning
external assistance through the provision of personnel and resources, already undertaken for mission countries or whole
continents, is only a first step in the direction of more radical
forms of renewal.

This brief analysis merely serves to indicate the basic functions of the Church as a social system and the mechanisms it
uses to fulfil them. It confirms our initial assumption that the
Church not only can change but does change, and it clearly
shows the urgency of modernizing the systems of control and
communication within the Church. But renewal is impossible
without active, structured participation. Institutional bottle-

necks or the cultural lag of particular persons or milieus are no justification for delay. We are too accustomed to use clemency and charity when we are afraid of responsibilities. Much hesitation, with consequent failure in moral duty, is due to vain hopes that others will change, that others will effect change, and so we spare ourselves the hard work of seeing, judging, and acting. The sense of possessing the privilege of truth and the fear of pursuing, concretizing, or even merely proclaiming it, whatever the cost, result in a paradox: a sterile expectation of the worst with a vague sense of comfort in the best which remains to us. We are thus condemned to live in the past and on the merits of the past instead of confessing our present weakness and rediscovering the torch of hope.

In practice, the need for systematic information is immediately apparent in the case of large-scale institutions. When society was such that man could acquire all the information he needed almost without effort, it was not necessary to systematize the flow of religious information except in ways pertinent and limited to the time in question. The catechism and periodic contact with the parish priest were sufficient to recall the principles of the faith and to clarify questions that had become more difficult with the passing of the years. It was a solid Catholicism precisely because it was closed and had no desire for encounter or conflict with the world or with other beliefs and religions.

Today the general climate is quite different. Constant communication between heads and members, among the leaders and members themselves, is indispensable for the external efficacy of the institution, that is, for the accomplishment of its goals, its mission. The aim of the Church is the orientation of men's minds through evangelization and a sanctifying action whose object is also mankind. The development of guiding principles requires systematic information on the most vital problems and emerging needs of modern man. The same is true for carrying out the salvific mission. The relation between the Church and the world, the continuing Incarnation, is impossible if the whole Church—as St. John says of Christ, who "knew what was in man" [John 2:25]—does not follow his example in the human terms proper to it.

Systematic information is equally necessary for the internal efficiency of the organization. In fact, changes in external situations require structural adaptation on the part of the institution. Since the laws of adaptation follow those of change, if there is a progressive sharpening of change, there must be a parallel development of adaptation so that it will not be achieved too late. Most delays in the Church are not due to reluctance so much as to lack of information, because the sources of information and the methods for gathering it are inadequate both in quantity and quality. The more complex and important an institution is, the more it is nourished by the voluntary thrust which ensures its dynamism and the more it needs—as a real, irreducible, and determining part of development itself—suitable mechanisms which anticipate the range and projects of renewal.

Notes

[1] P. Tufari, "Functional Analysis in the Sociology of Religion," in *Social Compass*, Vol. VII, No. 1 (1960), pp. 16–18.

[2] Tufari, *loc. cit.*, p. 15.

[3] Tufari, *loc. cit.*, pp. 15–16.

[4] E. Pin, *Pratique Religieuse et Classes Sociales* (Paris, 1956).

[5] Tufari, *loc. cit.*, p. 16.

[6] In *Social Compass,* Vol. VIII, No. 5 (1961), pp. 407–423.

[7] Cf. T. Parsons, R. F. Bales, and E. H. Shils, *Working Papers in the Theory of Action* (Glencoe, Free Press, 1953).

[8] Tufari, *loc. cit.*, p. 16.

FOUR

The World's Concept of Progress

IN ANALYZING THE CHANGES that have occurred in the world, especially in the last century, there is danger of bogging down in partial views and approximate judgments, so that the result lacks coherence and validity. On the other hand, any attempt to grasp some unitary aspect in the restless human events of recent years involves a return to a philosophy or theology of history, and this may amount to a positive inventory of what today's world is saying about itself. It is precisely the spirit of unity, however, that is more aspiration than existential reality.

Despite the risk of posing the question in exigent terms, it is necessary to consider certain traditional orientations, particularly the evolution of the concepts of progress and development. Taken as reflections of contemporary humanity's action and awareness, they provide a frame of reference for any positive analysis of the changes that have occurred or are taking place. The following pages do not attempt to offer value judgments on these concepts, but merely note their connection with the actual evolution of human society and the way in which, while contributing to its success, they have also furthered the gradual "reduction" in the broader ambit of human sciences to the point of crisis. If, in fact, these concepts dominated European thinking to the extent that any attempt to challenge them has been and still is considered paradox or heresy,[1] their supremacy has begun to come under serious attack within the last thirty years due to the thrust of the very achievements they undoubtedly stimulated and promoted when they did not actually generate them, especially in the Western world. In a creative chaos of dimensions never before experienced, the entire magma of human experience has again been subjected to debate and rendered uncertain. While this produces a sense of loss and bewilderment, it also gives rise to the anxious and watchful expectation of a new creation.

Discussing the concept of progress, Dawson writes:

Every period of civilization possesses certain characteristic ideas that are peculiarly its own. They express the mind of the society that has given them birth, no less than does the artistic style or the social institutions of the age. Yet so long as they are dominant, their unique and original character is never fully recognized, since they are accepted as principles of absolute truth and universal validity. They are looked on not as the popular ideas of the moment, but as eternal truths implanted in the very nature of things, and as self-evident in any kind of rational thinking.

Now the idea of Progress has occupied a position of this kind in the modern civilization of Western Europe. It has been far more than a philosophical opinion or the doctrine of a school, for it has permeated the whole mind of society from the leaders of thought down to the politicians and the men of business, who would be the first to proclaim their distrust of idealism and their hostility to abstract theorizing. . . .[2]

The idea of progress has permeated daily living and become an integral part of the intellectual baggage and ethical imperative of every individual and of all peoples; it is one of the real, if not explicitly acknowledged, basic values which govern modern conduct. But in the process it seems to have become impoverished, reduced more or less to a passive acceptance and almost compulsory assent in the face of an ineluctable process.

It is no longer associated with a faith in a grandiose evolutionary process, content with being welded into the gradual improvement of the material conditions of existence. In fact, the idea of progress penetrated the masses only when they began to feel the practical effects of the politico-social changes which originated in the revolutionary period. For this reason, while political technicians and social agitators—whose attention is concentrated on the immediate future—have always accepted and proclaimed the concept and have embarked on passionate attempts to give it reality, historians, anthropologists, and sociologists—who are more concerned with tracing the actual curve of human evolution—restored the whole idea to more realistic dimensions and subjected it to searching criticism. Hence appropriate conclusions are now beginning to be drawn from the whole series of upheavals and pertinent studies which, as Dawson says, have undermined our faith in the unity of history.

This redimensioning of the idea of progress obeyed the normal laws of history. Taken by themselves, however, these could immobilize us in a dilemma: whether or not, given "historical necessity," the future is an open field for man's action. We would maintain, rather, that the concept was diminished by the real divorce which took place some centuries ago between science and social values, and we would draw attention to some key points which seem to have been neglected by historians of the idea, who have not given sufficient thought to its origin and social repercussions or to its connections with other operative factors in human experience.

In the common, generic acceptance of the term, progress means the process of amelioration and perfectioning both of the individual and of humanity. Implicit in the idea, therefore, is the conviction that the world is getting better every day in every way. When first introduced, the concept included a distinction between that which is immutable and that which evolves. In fact, St. Vincent of Lerins established a definite distinction between the concept of *profectus* (progress, development) and *permutatio* (change, alteration, deformation)— a distinction between a positive growth from within a reality which is permanent and filled with potential, and the external changes and erosions typical of nonspiritual natures.

This derivation of the term is unquestionably concerned with the theological controversies over the development and immutability of dogma and, therefore, with a particular meaning given the expression and language used to refer to the deposit of faith and, even more specifically, with the problem of making explicit what is implicit in dogma. Now it is well to note how all theological controversies come back in the end to the sense of history. The controversy of St. Vincent of Lerins with St. Augustine developed on much more serious fundamental differences involving the action of God and of man in history. It is therefore necessary to go back to the Christian origins of the idea of progress; these are closely related to the first true theology of history, which came into being with Christian thought.

We do not find the idea of progress among ancient peoples, particularly among the Greeks, for their knowledge of the world was determined by certain life situations and a mental climate that rendered it impossible. The concept of Fate gave rise to a cyclic view of history, and it is well-known that at the basis of pre-Christian cosmologies and cosmogonies, there is usually the theory of eternal recurrence, though with varying gradations in meaning and degree of emphasis. The ancient Greeks "possessed at that stage no history of their own past or of any other people, and so could not look back over a long course of events through which they had ascended or at least seemed to have ascended, as can modern nations rich in the records of their own past."[3] Even references to the Golden Age never had a real influence on their conception of history.

With its concept of creation, giving time and space a well-defined meaning, Christianity introduced the idea of progress. The idea of the unity of the world, governed by laws ultimately traceable to the action of Providence, to one source of

every beginning and one ultimate end of every activity, undoubtedly was also largely responsible for the concept of
natural law—at least as a working hypothesis, the fruitfulness
of which was and still is stressed by scientists. By Christian
view of history, we mean that which is rooted in the Hebrew
tradition and nourished by the Scriptures. The Hebrews, in
fact, are the only people of the ancient world to possess a history written in anticipation of and prefiguring the course they
should follow in establishing a close relationship with their
God. The prophecies and other writings with a Messianic
background permeated for many centuries the life and institutions of Israel and constituted the source for the historic understanding and justification of the life and work of Christ. We
might even add that wherever expectations of the dawn of a
new era were widespread, especially in the East and during the
Augustan age, they were due in large measure to the Messianic expectation of the Hebrews which was carried throughout
the Diaspora.

Within the context of this fundamental but quite clear view
of history, whose greatest exponent is St. Augustine, it is possible to note several of the more specific concepts which suc-
cessively provided a point of reference for the theory of evolution—as, for example, St. Augustine's *rationes seminales,* understood as secondary causes whose potentiality is not manifest
but becomes so in the course of time.

The Middle Ages witnessed a deepening of the Christian
concept and, in fact, the development of the premises for the
later series of motivations and incentives which led to the explosion of the idea of progress in modern times. The Golden

Age meanwhile was transformed into the far-off Eden, and the idea of original sin was restated in the broader vision of the Redemption and the Divine Providence which governs history. On this subject Gilson writes:

The idea of progressive change . . . was formulated in the most forcible manner by St. Augustine and those Christian thinkers he inspired. It was new; neither in Plato, nor in Aristotle, not even in the Stoics, do we find the now so familiar notion of humanity conceived as an unique collective being, made up more of dead than living, always in progress towards a perfection, drawing ever nearer and nearer. Ordered and penetrated through and through by an internal finality, almost we might say by an unique *intention,* the succession of generations in time has not only a real unity, but, being now offered to thought as something more than an accidental succession of events, it acquires an intelligible meaning; and therefore, even if the Middle Ages is to be taxed with a lack of historical sense, we must at least grant it the merit of assisting at the birth of a philosophy of history. Nay, more, let us say that it had one, and that in so far as it still exists, our own is more penetrated with medieval and Christian principles than we usually imagine.[4]

Against the general historical background, each human being's history proceeds from infancy to old age, as he accumulates knowledge and grows in his capacity to learn and to act. As expressed by Gilson,

When eventually he vanishes from the scene his efforts are not on that account lost, for what is true of individuals is true also of societies that survive them, and of intellectual and moral disciplines which survive the societies themselves. For this reason . . . there is a progress in the political and social order, just as there is in the intellectual order of science and philosophy, each new generation becoming the beneficiary of all the truths accumulated by its predecessors, profiting even by their very errors and transmitting a growing heritage to posterity. . . . For this reason the Christian thinkers would naturally come to conceive . . . that the entire human race, whose life resembles that of a single man, passes from Adam till the end of the world through a series of successive states, grows old in regular sequence, laying up meanwhile a store of natural and supernatural knowledge until it shall attain the perfect age, which shall be that of its future glory.[5]

It is easy to see how the medieval concept included the attempt to define the stages or phases through which human history passes.[6] In particular, the Augustinian notion of the progress of the human race as if it were a single being is applied to the growth of human knowledge by St. Bonaventure, even though in terms of mankind's progress toward its supernatural end. Pascal later extended this application to the progressive mastery of the sciences through man's work in any field.

In the Oxford School, moreover, this aspect of progress was stressed by Duns Scotus (*in processu generationis humanae semper crevit notitia veritatis*). Roger Bacon emphasized that the temporal succession of generations is not only biological change but brings with it a richer and more certain heritage than that discovered and preserved by the ancients, and in this he is the forerunner of Giordano Bruno and Francis Bacon.

With Humanism and the Renaissance came the thrust toward humanizing the view of history. Moving away from the concept of Providence, which makes itself known in more or less definable cycles according to a superior logic unknown to man, the new view reflected a clear tendency to humanize the concept of man, centering it in his reason. By putting man at the center of reality, the Renaissance revolution slowly opened the way to the idea of evolution and of inner laws which animate and permeate with a transforming influence man's journey in the world, amid the various processes of fluctuation and differentiation. The religious context became progressively weaker as man gained mastery over the secrets and forces of nature, and the concept of "managing" nature itself, through science and technology, took hold with the evocative power of a myth.

This transformation in mentality, sketched here only briefly, was undoubtedly furthered by a number of fundamental convictions which arose and took root over the centuries but which finally merged into a terrestrial revision—if we may call it so—of human progress. Time and space lost its sacral character, and in a certain sense the significance of mankind's forward progress was also secularized. We shall now attempt to determine some of the mediating elements which accelerated the transformation, although—since we are dealing with cultural and social factors—it is not possible to fix the precise time when they were operative because the period between their appearance and their actual assimilation in the social patrimony cannot be defined.

The first of these influences was undoubtedly Francis

Bacon's "usefulness of learning." This usefulness increases, because learning—which is or ought to be positive—is in the process of development as opposed to "given" or "innate" knowledge. The usefulness concept was undoubtedly influenced by the interminable and ineffectual nominalist quarrels of the late Middle Ages and by the rise of a merchant and industrial class in England, which for the first time used learning to practical advantage in social terms.

It is easy to see how the English empirical tradition led to studies of human behavior, first analyzed in terms of individual knowledge and then studied in terms of social existence and action, with the discovery of the laws governing human relationships. This current of thought met, if indeed it did not produce, the rise of the applied sciences which transferred investigation of the Baconian "nature" of phenomena to societal life and which stimulated research even on the "natural laws" of human behavior over and above the inexhaustible variety of its manifestations.

Another very important influence in the development of the idea of progress was the conviction—already full-blown at the beginning of the Renaissance and reinforced in suceeding periods—that since man is capable of imitating the great personages of the past, he is quite capable of reshaping his own future. This heady impulse found concrete confirmation in the growing and increasingly organized expression of the scientific spirit, which gradually became scientific conviction. As Dawson rightly observes, the excitement of the "great century" did not blossom forth all of a sudden. Judgment on preceding ages was rooted in the "literary culture of the Renaissance, which revived in an abstract form the old dualism between Hellenism and barbarism and thus for the first time introduced a cleavage between the facts of social development and the ideals of the educated classes."[7] This has received little attention in studies on the origins of the idea of progress. The secularization of learning reproduced the separation between Hellenes and barbarians within the circles of society considered advanced and "civilized," so that the new clerics took upon themselves the duty and right, not only of interpretation, but even of representing the "people" altogether. It is not without reason that from the end of the Renaissance, spontaneous popular reaction found expression in apocalyptic and revolutionary movements which met with no adequate response in the thinking and interests of the educated classes. The separation became more acute in the course of time when the latter, in addition to their monopoly on learning and representation, gradually joined forces with the owners of the means of production and concentrated their energies on the scientific-technical knowledge required for the exploitation of resources. This distinction, expressed colloquially in the antithesis "poor man–gentleman," spread from the cultural to the social field, increasingly aggravated by reciprocal reactions and resentments. In the colonial experience, the ruling class saw, not a term of comparison, but social affirmation of the conviction of its own superiority, and this is still at the root of the "ethnocentrism" which tends to mar all discussion on the development of backward societies.

Cartesianism undoubtedly gave this conviction of superiority a thrust forward. Writes Dawson:

The originality of Descartes consisted rather in his complete divorce of the human mind as a thinking substance from any dependence on, or even any apparent relation to, the body which it informs and the conditions of physical existence with which it appears to be bound up. The human reason without recourse either to experience or to authority is able to deduce an absolutely certain and complete knowledge from the clear and simple truths which are innate in its own being and which it comprehends by a direct act of intuition. . . . This unbounded faith in the power of Reason is manifested in all that the philosophers of the 18th century wrote concerning social and political questions. Above all, the conception of social progress, as elaborated by the Abbé de St. Pierre, Turgot and Condorcet, was almost exclusively intellectual. . . .[8]

These different mediating influences necessarily resulted in a revision of the philosophy of history. This was now detached from the strictly Christian matrix from which it had sprung, and it drew upon new types of knowledge and experience which the discovery of the new world and new social structures were accumulating. Thus, in the evolution of the progress concept, interpretations of universal history—and especially that of Bodin—assumed a growing and determining importance. As G. Bouthoul points out, contact with other peoples and other histories through geographical discoveries furthered the trend in this direction.[9] Events in Europe reinforced the belief in a single rational civilization, in its excellence, and consequently in the legitimacy of a hierarchic classification of societies on the basis of this unchallengeable standard of comparison. While, on the one hand, this led to the first acquisition of social science—namely, the concept of relativism, which was gradually developed through the comparative method—on the other, it lent first contacts with other cultures an attitude whose limitations and poverty are still evident today. Since one type of civilization was producing more power, wealth, well-being, and justice than all the others, it was assumed that the latter would sooner or later move toward it.

In the writings of acknowledged standard-bearers of the idea of progress—Montesquieu, Condorcet, Saint-Simon, Comte, Marx,—it is easy to observe how the thrust of positivism and the radical changes resulting from the Industrial Revolution gradually introduced the criterion of social efficiency into the concept of progress itself. The idea was, in fact, reduced to the tangible proofs offered by the full and continuous application of scientific laws. Since the search at this time was for a positive and scientific basis for the fundamental ideas of the preceding period, the social efficiency reflected in these tangible proofs gave the economic factor a decisive importance even in the theoretic explanations of progress. Economics was directly linked to the scientific-technical factor, and it could offer the most conclusive evidence of human advancement precisely because of the structure which production was gradually assuming. It may therefore be argued that in the late 18th and early 19th centuries the concept of progress was strengthened both by the impressive evidence of technology and by the increasing influence of positivist philosophy on the mentality of particular social groups. The scientific synthesis attempted by the authors mentioned above was essentially sociological: it led to the conclusion that nature was to be interpreted in social terms and was no longer to be considered a broader whole of which society is but one part and on which it depends. Pragmatism, vitalism, and an ingenuous materialism gradually dethroned the intellect from its original position of uncontested supremacy. Since the possibility of an absolutely valid synthesis was rejected, the dualism between human values and external nature could be resolved only by the complete subordination of thought to the human goals which were socially attainable and were most useful with respect to both time and methods. Comte considered that the function of science was to serve humanity, and he condemned research undertaken as an end in itself. The *cogitatio* and free, contemplative vision of the true, therefore, were rejected; and technology was increasingly exalted as the intensified extension into the world of all that man succeeds in building in his Herculean efforts to combat and conquer its forces. The discipline which, in the midst of this enthusiasm, first succeeded in deducing laws and discovering proof of its accuracy and perfectibility gained ground over every other branch of knowledge.

As for the influence of the technological factor on the power groups—mentioned above as playing an essential part in modifying the idea of progress—technology as a mental and social attitude resulted, of itself, in a change of values. Originally the idea of progress derived from a certain philosophy of history and, consequently, a global vision of human advancement. Under the influence of knowledge orientated to and by technology, the notion of value and of progress in history was reduced to nothing other than movement in time and space.

The old and the outmoded lacked value. Technology, by its very nature, was the most progressive element.

This habit of mind, which gradually identified progress with economic development, was determined by the close relationship between science and technology. We usually start with the premise that the goal of science is knowledge and that of technology is action. In reality, science and technology, in the sense of social or instrumental technique, pursue the same goals: knowledge and action. Moreover, there is no distinction between them in the degree of intellectual commitment which creates them; a distinction can be made only with respect to the levels on which they develop. Science is essentially a system of elaborating abstract concepts; technology, essentially a system of relationships among various acts when it is social, and among material bodies when it is instrumental.

This identity of goals is in itself a product of history, of human experience. It has been accentuated by the trend toward social utilization of intellectual effort, which came to maturity with the birth of the social sciences as an extension of the natural sciences. It was the success of instrumental techniques that restricted science to a utilitarian perspective and led to the view that the only true science was that which could be demonstrated by concrete proofs achieved through controlled studies or experiments. It is unquestionably true that scientific theories are genuine intellectual instruments for discovering reality, genuine attempts to establish and express the interrelationships between the system of abstract concepts (which is science) and the system of concrete phenomena (which is reality). But it is also true, and in fact inevitable, that the inter-relationships between concepts and phenomena which are more "evident" through the direct medium of action than through the logical connection of categories assume much more prominence. Experimentation and large-scale application eventually dominate the current mental outlook and influence the very aims of mental effort. Utility wins out over the disinterested drudgery of pure research.

The shattering effect on society of this solid thought-action complex is so great that techniques of a purely intellectual order have no influence except after the shock produced by the effectiveness of purely material techniques. Take, for example, the value assumed by war since the beginning of the century. Rather than a means of imposing a rule or defending a right, it is a manifestation of the superior equipment and organization of the society which engages in it. When we consider, on the historical level, that the technical complex always corresponds to a well-defined human area, that it produces a serious (however slow and fragmentary) modification of the instrumental elements of family and social life, that it transforms individual and group sentiments, that it generates strong reactions in spiritual life and leads to syncretisms that go beyond the traditional mentality—when we consider all this, we can appreciate the efficacy attained by technology in the society which preceded us and the fact that it was assimilated to the point of dominating the global view of human advancement, that is, the idea of progress.

Only recently has the conviction grown that technical change is a consequence of social change, that the perception of time,

space, distance, speed, and other realities in a given group is
governed by the convictions of the group. Today reality is
considered a function of culture, and many data are considered
to be determined by the changes taking place in the culture.
At the beginning of the first Industrial Revolution, however,
the machine and other data were thought to be both the efficient and the final causes of progress. Scholars who attempted
to reconsider the concept of progress and to establish criteria
for its evaluation or categories for its constants were overcome
by the spontaneous fact, by this prodigy in which everything
or nothing could be resolved, but which was, nevertheless, a
source of hope and a basis for the difficult structure of social
life. This fact, which paradoxically led to the mechanistic
character of the first economic and sociological constructions,
was not marked by social awareness as the pivot of progress.
Mankind was too fascinated by the work of its own hands to
notice the determining importance of collective responsibility.
But, as Nordskog comments,

Dewey says, progress depends, not on the existence of social change,
but on the direction which human beings deliberately give to that
change. . . . the ease of social change is a condition of progress . . .
while the modern man was deceived about the amount of progress he
had made, and especially deceived about the automatic certainty
of progress, he was right in thinking that for the first time in history
mankind is in command of the possibility of progress. The future
of progress depends upon man to say whether he wants it or not.
Progress must be conceived as a responsibility, not as an endow-
ment. But, if progress is to have its chance, certain conservative

attitudes which propagate disbelief in the possibility of constructive social engineering will have to yield to or at least be tempered by attitudes.[10]

Notes

[1] Cf. C. Dawson, *Progress and Religion* (New York, Sheed & Ward, 1938).

[2] *Ibid.,* p. 3.

[3] C. M. Case, "Progress: A Western Notion", in J. E. Nordskog, *Social Change* (New York, McGraw-Hill, 1960), p. 129.

[4] E. Gilson, *The Spirit of Medieval Philosophy,* trans. by A. H. Downes (New York, Scribner, 1936), pp. 389–390.

[5] *Ibid.,* pp. 388–389.

[6] On the function of medieval thought in developing the idea of progress, see A. Comte, *Système de Politique Positive* (Paris, 1912), Vol. 2, p. 116 ff.

[7] Dawson, *op. cit.,* p. 10.

[8] *Ibid.,* pp. 11–12.

[9] Cf. G. Bouthoul, *Traité de Sociologie,* Vol. I (Paris, 1949), pp. 504–505; Vol. II (1954), p. 21 ff.

[10] J. E. Nordskog, *Social Change* (New York, McGraw-Hill, 1960), p. 154. Copyright © 1960 by McGraw-Hill, Inc. Used by permission of McGraw-Hill Book Company.

FIVE

The World's Concept of Development

OUR REFLECTIONS on the evolution of the idea of progress, while noting the changes, confirm the fact that this idea constitutes an irreplaceable patrimony of modern human behavior. If we stressed its "reduction" in the broader field of human experience, it was only to conclude that every product of the past must be consciously interiorized to ensure its true development. Since the idea of progress has gradually become identified with the theory of economic development, it is well to note how the concept of development has evolved in recent years and how it has been extended to a series of experiences since the beginning of this century.[1]

The phenomenon of underdevelopment has been a conspicuous and tragic exception in the process of economic expansion brought about first by the thrust of colonialism and then by the need to preserve the high standards of productivity imposed by the new technology. Since it affected the survival of two-thirds of mankind, this phenomenon could no longer be set aside in accordance with the traditional theory, even if some fundamental categories pertinent to that theory were to be jeopardized. War abundantly demonstrated that the scientific organization of production is possible through political action aimed at the full exploitation of natural resources and manpower. Hence the task of those entrusted with the destiny of people is not to find the means to an end so much as to define the end itself. Finally, a collective consciousness of this idea of growth asserted itself in the form of human progress toward an *ideal* beyond history, or as history's final goal. This consciousness is collective in that it is not so much the result of knowledge produced by the philosophy of the enlightenment as it is the outcome of *social awareness*. Man has discovered—through his dominion over nature, which he exercises in association with his fellows—the decisive importance of the group, the masses, the attitudes and ideas of the community. Thus all the resurgent Messianic doctrines are not collective projections of individuals utopias, as in the past, but rather a historic consequence of experiences shared in common in the technological world. These experiences are had within cultural areas endowed with richer resources and inventiveness, or they are learned through the various means of communication which ensure a constant exchange between person and person, people and people.

This awareness of the realities which promote concern for economic development, however, has also brought to light profound ambiguities. The definition of indexes, factors, and causes which affect economic expansion is still uncertain, confused, and sometimes even contradictory. The ever-growing complexity of structural forms in the various societies has helped to cancel out deterministic explanations in the search for factors and causes. Despite attempts in the recent past to provide a clear and unanimous answer, the results have been scanty. We may, however, discern three trends of thought.

First, some have used the term "economic development" to indicate certain specific changes affecting various aspects of structures or of socioeconomic dynamics (industrialization, agrarian reform, cultural modernization, etc.) For them these changes represent only a tactical phase within a truly global and harmonious development of society, the definition of which is carefully avoided.

Secondly, there are those who have concentrated their attention on long-term objectives of a global character within the growth-process. They have attempted to point out certain goals toward which the evolution of society, which they consider a complex and historically determined organism, must converge. In this category fall all the disputes on centrally controlled planning, as well as the actual plan and values which are to guide the elaboration and achievement of this total goal beyond the purely technical stage.

Thirdly, there are still others, who, at a completely different level, have tried to grasp in every economic growth-process the ultimate meaning of human history, seeking through value-judgments and a specific philosophical perspective the ultimate principle of all historical processes and, finally, a philosophy or theology of history. In this category fall all discussions of cultural nationalism, imperialism, and what might be called "applied Teilhardism."

It is a well-known fact that the existential conditions in which some of these theories of economic development were elaborated have unquestionably changed. Furthermore, human experience has created crisis, on the historical and mental levels, in all that man believed he had acquired once and for all. A first observation is suggested by the everyday use of the word "development." It indicates an advance toward the *ideal,* which ceases when the *ideal goal* has been reached. To take man as an example, we consider an individual's growth to be an advance toward his full stature, strength, capacity for action, intellectual maturity, and moral life. Where man is concerned, however, there is no ideal in an absolute sense; for the complexity of his body and of his psyche demonstrates that only relative and successive goals exist for him. This means that the growth-concept is already complex with respect to the individual, and it becomes still more complex when we consider him as a part of social organisms (family, group, Church, State). We must then take into account all the notions drawn by human experience from long compliance with and codification of the laws regulating the static and dynamic social structure. Thus, on the basis of daily observation, we can distinguish two ways of understanding the complex concept of economic expansion: mechanical and organic. In the mechanical approach the goals (or the *ideal*) are quantitative. They can be determined beforehand and attained with certainty, for the time and means for their achievement can be determined scientifically.

This basic dualism, which also parallels a general attitude toward life and history, explains the confusion in present-day literature on economic development. We may note therein the use of expressions whose broader meanings are ambiguously narrowed, while other limited expressions, whose meaning is by definition purely methodological, are used in a much broader sense. Undoubtedly the organic concept of development has proved to be more valid, and the term has become very popular in the literature devoted to collective aspirations. Currently the term "economic development" is not confined to only one aspect of reality, even the economic, because mankind's experience has hastened the integration of the various disciplines by exposing the ingenuousness of attempting to formulate an abstract science which would have a universal application. Hence it is necessary to take into account an ever-increasing number of factors in order to identify those orientations which favor an orderly and continuous growth. This is what is meant by organic economic growth.[2]

To what can we attribute this substantial change in the concept of growth, particularly with respect to the thinking responsible for its initial and fundamental success? The word "growth" has appeared in the terminology of economics as a special expression of the dynamic theory, an economic doctrine wherein time is considered an essential factor. Time is considered the variable on which depend different economic quantities. In the theory of economic development, the essential character of time changes qualitatively. "Time is viewed as the dimension in which a human activity (human in the real sense of the word) takes place; that is, an activity that creates a sequence of events, each of which is qualitatively new and irreducible to the preceding ones. Hence this is an activity which, in the course of time, produces processes characterized not simply by the variation of determinate quantities but essentially by the movements toward new positions that are always qualitatively different."[3]

Not so long ago economists developed their theories in a world in which the time factor was not integrated in economic analysis, in a world lacking true temporality. The *homo oeconomicus* thought he was endowed with a perfect rationality and would move in an eternal present.[4] Classical economists, on the other hand, had reduced all analysis of development to the study of progression toward the state of equilibrium. Although accepting the distinction between the short-term and the long-term period, they put aside the problem of change that takes place from one period to another (together with the problems inherent in the relationships which determine the structural changes in growth) in order to uphold the elements on which the abstract notion of equilibrium used to depend. The movements which take place during the very long-term period are "brought about by the gradual development of technological know-how, population, capital and . . . the changing conditions on which supply and and demand depend from generation to generation."[5] Given its characteristics, it is easy to see how this period was foreign to economic analysis.[6] Confined to such a period, economic development did not seem to be the object of scientific analysis.[7]

In its rigorous logic, economic analysis rejected the pressures arising from social forces or from numerous social problems.

It thus was inevitably orientated toward efficiency-science, which considered foreign those peculiarly human variables (whether of the individual or the group) which are not reducible to, or compatible with, quantities which can be analyzed by means of a rational method. Always more attractive, partiality was accepted as both the point of departure and frame of reference in the study of social behavior in order to assure the logical rigor of the discipline and the rejection of utopias. With Marx and Schumpeter, however, the problem of organic growth is directly or indirectly faced by introducing variables formerly neglected or considered not subject to economic analysis. This introduction of new elements—to which were later added variations arising from the historical context, political experience, and "mental universes"—prompted the gradual transition from economic theory to growth theory.

It should be noted, however, that the Marxist theory deals with the problem of economic development by concentrating on capitalism. Because of the importance it gives the accumulation of capital, it remains very close to classical thought, but it nevertheless makes a fundamental departure in considering this accumulation nothing but a variable dependent on sociological factors. In fact, the Marxist theory of the economic growth-process is founded on the behavior and strategy of a social group, and it implies in its development a transformation of the sociological data affecting production. The power of entrepreneurs over the economy and society through private ownership of the means of production prevents harmonious growth, but remains, paradoxically, the source of its dynamism. The accumulation of individual and social capital depends on the capitalization of the profit-value, which is closely bound to the behavior of capitalist entrepreneurs as well as to the pertinent institutional framework.

Economic growth takes place only in a sociologically stable environment. As the growth-process is realized, the environment is modified, and the modification reacts on the growth-process itself. Thus the Marxist theory demonstrates the fundamental importance of sociological and institutional factors to balanced economic growth. By introducing an endogenous factor—the tendency to lower profit—the Marxist economic principle explains the arrest of capitalistic growth and the collapse of the State. However, in emphasizing the importance of sociological factors within the growth-process, the Marxist theory rejected spontaneous equilibrium, even if it formulated a series of categories which today do not bear scientific criticism. In problems of underdevelopment, therefore, the Marxist theory has been unable to foresee the logic of other factors, and so has applied a seemingly rigid and abstract scheme outside the historical context which occasioned it.

Schumpeter shows a keen sense of the dimensions which affect economic growth in relation to man's direct action. The idea of innovation is the central point in Schumpeter's vision. The growth-factor is identified with an element within the system, the manifestation of which is unforeseeable: the *innovation*. This innovation is intrinsic in the system, for it acts upon the production-data combination, whatever its form may be: new products, new energy, new method, new market, new organization of industry. Once it has appeared, innovation upsets the system and gives rise to a "creative destruction" in which old relationships and structures are demolished. In Schumpeter's view man's direct responsibility in the growth-process lies in the fact that the innovator, the dynamic entre-preneur—though he represents the technological factor—is always the expression of a society or of a series of social habits.

By following the main lines of Schumpeter's theory, it is easy to proceed to analysis of the sociocultural environment that characterizes innovation, the original and creative value of which is otherwise unjustifiable. Even though developed within our Western framework, these two sample analyses indicate some of the elements which, as part of the patrimony of economic thought, are important for a regular and more concrete discussion of the dynamics of economic development. These were not at first followed up. When reference was made to them in more recent times, historical experience revealed not only their validity but also their limitations. Although dynamic, they could not include all the factors manifest in the phenomenon of underdevelopment. It is precisely this phe-nomenon which has brought the theory of economic growth to a crisis.

To discuss the concept of underdevelopment correctly, we must avoid the mistaken premise that one set of economies is in frantic motion, the other completely static. This error is usually made by those who limit themselves to economic terminology. Instead, we must recognize the dynamism pe-culiar to underdeveloped societies, which becomes even more evident when they are compared with the developed societies and which raises totally different problems in the field of political knowledge and action. The structures of the economic

and social systems being compared must be regarded, therefore, as *dynamic,* even if we grant them an intrinsic "margin
of autonomy"[8] and a profound differentiation in the manner
in which they operate and evolve. This preliminary observation must be thoroughly examined.

The dynamism of underdeveloped societies does not appear to be directly conditioned by aspiration to an ever-increasing possession of material goods. Nor does it necessarily evolve
according to the patterns followed by industrial societies. The
transforming powers, Balandier observes, do not always aim
at the betterment of the material conditions of life, for well-
being is not always their objective. The solution of problems
which arise from underdevelopment requires a particular
readjustment of internal dynamism. This is almost impossible
without an ideological change capable of putting sociological
agents into new orbits, since depression often forces even
ideals into passive fatalism. This spiritual readiness is rendered
more urgent by the rhythm of sociological and technological
change. The spread of new methods of production, the reversal
in the play of inner and outward forces with regard to traditional economies, the tendency to individualize both revenues
and utilization of wealth, the rise of the competitive function
in relations of pure exchange and reciprocity, the transformation of social functions and sociocultural environments—all
these impose unavoidable choices. Meanwhile, the rhythm of
individual and social life must be adjusted to new aesthetic,
ethical, and logical patterns.[9]

Every outside intervention in an underdeveloped zone becomes a real dilemma; consequently, the conception itself of

economic development is profoundly conditioned. Technological efficiency, rationality, and positiveness in the structure and culture of industrialized societies all run up against the scepticism of underdeveloped societies where ethics and values are concerned. If the structures and forms of developed societies represent the result of the reciprocal influence of the two factors, how can one be established without the other? Since the sociological aspect of economic growth seems to find its natural completion in meeting human needs, is growth—in the common meaning of the term—necessarily bound up with the concept of welfare, as this is understood by some Western societies? For example, let us consider the innovating function, which Schumpeter envisaged as the flywheel of growth:

The problem of economic growth related to areas outside the capitalistic markets is . . . that of creating a productive system sufficiently integrated *in a short time* rather than gradually, as was the case with those economies which, during the nineteenth century, became industrialized by stages. Actually, the problem originates from the fact that in already industrialized countries, the *ex post* coordination of investments must take place through the *increments* of productive capacity and involves a relatively modest share of the national capital; but in countries where the industrialization-process is just beginning, this coordination must, instead, take place through *initial* investments, each of which is a relevant share of the still modest national capital. Since this is the picture within which decisions to invest are to be arrived at in underdeveloped countries, the often-repeated tenet that the industrialization processes are unlikely to take place in those countries because they do not possess the categories once present in and favorable to the industrialization of the developed countries seems to be unjustified if based on this circumstance alone.

Entrepreneurs, and those who are likely to become such, find themselves making decisions on investments in underdeveloped countries in circumstances totally different from those surrounding the pioneers of the first industries. The picture indeed differs because of the increased difficulties in modern technological procedures and because of the competition encountered by the newly developed countries in the markets in which they must operate. And we cannot see any ground for the belief that the creators of the first industries could repeat their undoubtedly great experience in an underdeveloped country if this were simply able to offer them the institutional framework in which they successfully operated in their time.[10]

Hence the global, extremely rapid, and rigidly technical character of the intervention in underdeveloped areas in order to start the growth-process calls for new approaches in an economic setting which is quite different from that characteristic of developed societies. Economic analysis, if it is to be realistic, "must deal with all the relevant factors; the general economic theory must become social theory."[11]

After Adam Smith, works on political economy have developed the idea that consumption is the only end of production, but in actual life this concept has never played an essential role. The essential objective was production in view of immediate profits while this production was not at all the basic preoccupation of the State . . . Any parliamentary document picked at random in any developed country, originating during this initial period of industrialization, will reveal a terminology as well as an ideology totally different from the terminology and ideology that nowadays characterize the growth of underdeveloped countries.[12]

National and political effort which promotes economic growth is a new phenomenon. The choice of methods is, of course, influenced by political, ideological, and social factors that emphasize or minimize the seriousness of the need. The problem of growth, however, can never be reduced to one of economic technology. The assimilation of methods tested elsewhere cannot be a substitute for a global vision of the economy or of a society where growth is beginning or is being encouraged.

From another point of view, evaluation of the initial stage of economic growth, once relations among different economies have been established, is often upset by periods of change which destroy the remnants of politico-historical order and accelerate their disintegration. The traditional theory proves inadequate to offset the resulting imbalance. It was never interested in problems wherein there is a marked difference between the various methods of production, corresponding to extremely important differences in the pertinent scarcity of factors as well as to great differences in the living levels within the sociocultural system and, particularly, within the institutional framework. Traditional theory—while admitting the existence of two orders, economic and noneconomic— always held that only the interrelationship in the economic order could be rationally analyzed. Myrdal holds that it is "precisely within the realm of this large section of the social sphere neglected by economic analysis in its abstraction from the noneconomic factors that the assumed balance lacks stability. These noneconomic factors cannot be considered as static data; when they act, their reaction is normally one of imbalance."[13] The conclusion to be drawn is obvious.

If other, noneconomic factors—administrative efficiency, health factors, degree of education, incentives and motives governing behavior—must be invoked (in addition to those the traditional theory recognizes as economic) in order to make the economic growth-process in an underdeveloped country intelligible, the science of economics is likely to be stretched too far—even to the point of becoming a different type of analysis which, in the broad sense, could be called sociological. We cannot assume a process of growth based only on the economy.

Stimulated by the phenomenon of underdevelopment, the rethinking of economic theory has been accelerated by a series of factors:

(a) the growing political importance of underdeveloped countries, with the rise of nationalism and the emergence—more or less marked at the ideological level—of the "third world" in the dialectic of blocs;

(b) the failure of technical assistance in some underdeveloped countries, because insufficient consideration was given to the characteristics of the society for which it was destined and, particularly, to the degree of sociocultural preparedness to receive it;

(c) the necessity for innovations, without destroying the

traditional values which govern the life of the community to be assisted;

(d) the increasing necessity for national and local communities to participate in economic development in order to ensure the organic advancement of all their members at the civic level;

(e) the need to avoid political upheavals (capable of subverting the entire framework of social forces) and to take into account the ideological components and the institutional picture in which such forces express themselves and oppose one another;

(f) the growing tendency in all underdeveloped countries to formulate long-range plans, which create vast problems of personnel and cultural organization in general.

Under the influence of all these factors, economic literature on development has been enriched by a series of studies on the social and cultural aspects of economic development. Critical analysis of intergovernmental activity in this field has yielded further results of an operational order. Research has been undertaken to pinpoint the sociocultural problems connected with change, or with obstacles to change, in the social structures or cultural values of various societies. This research has led to the identification of a social-cultural world—to a certain extent autonomous or subject to laws of a different kind—which surrounds and influences economic decisions and may jeopardize their effectiveness.

The theory of underdevelopment, far from being a rehash of the growth theory, has proved to be a theory of intercultural influences among societies at different levels of technical development, which studies the specific sociocultural changes resulting from their contacts.

The way has thus been cleared for consideration of the value system that may resist change. The difficulties encountered by instrumental technology, when introduced into underdeveloped societies, are recognized *a priori* as originating from the attitudes or motivations of individuals and groups deriving from their scale of values. Any growth-promoting action risks failure unless new values are introduced into the existing sociocultural context. It is not a question of replacing existing attitudes with others, but rather of being able to check their effects (whether functional or dysfunctional) and the connection between certain attitudes and motivations structurally and dynamically integrated in social life. These attitudes and motivations—including those which relate to economic activity—may be functional or dysfunctional, with regard to growth, depending on the sociocultural context in which they are operative and the process which gave rise to them in individual and social habits.[14] As a final result, so-called "Western ethnocentrism"—whereby economic development was considered an extension or application of what was thought to be the superior Western model—has been abandoned.

Another series of studies has been done on the incidence of innovation by entrepreneurs, the role of bureaucracy, the importance of the individuals or groups manifesting resistance to change, and the strategy of growth. These studies are conducted on an increasingly empirical basis, under pressure of the varied needs and marked differences in the societies in which action for growth is taking place or is being planned.

We have come, therefore, to a revision of the theory of economic development for reasons which may seem external but are substantially of an interior order. The classical picture did not prove adequate to include a theory of economic expansion, just as the capitalist economy has not proved historically capable of expanding beyond the originally industrialized countries. We could find a sort of historical justification for the first series of reasons; for the second, the reasons are actual and pressing. Through a fundamental evolution, the economy has been changing from an economy of want to an economy of wealth; this is the radically new fact since World War II.

Economic science, which gradually became the science of economic development, finalized its contribution to maintaining and increasing the increment rate of income and faithfully accepted the myth of production. This finalization, accepted as *obvious,* is now in crisis because of the very process by which a wealthy society has been formed. Economic theory had begun with an examination of producer and consumer behavior in an environmental scarcity of material goods and, therefore, had concentrated attention on problems related to increasing production and to satisfying the need for goods. With the passing of time, however, the situation changed. The ability of the systems of industrialized countries to ensure the full employment of productive factors and resources (under markedly economical conditions, coupled with high and steadily increasing levels of income and consumption) has sidetracked the problems of production and consumption.

To an ever-increasing degree, these problems are entrusted to experts in production and marketing. The science of organization has prevailed over that of need.

Meanwhile, we have also become aware of the rise of new forces, motivations, and elements within the same economic framework. Strictly speaking, their evaluation was not within the domain either of economic analysis or of the new technocratic methods. The constantly extended and intensified action of public enterprise along with integrated private units, the actual type of market growth characterized by production structures sometimes strikingly different from those of free competition, the decreasing atomism in decisions with respect to supply and demand, the increasing emergence within industrialized countries of requirements and needs which were either inadequately filled or (even if still latent) could not be considered less pressing—all these factors have posed economic questions whose solution cannot depend on a criterion based on *economic theory itself,* and, least of all, on one of efficiency.

Consumption always seems to be more of an independent social variable than a function of production. From Smith to Ricardo, from Malthus to Marx, a general and progressive want had been the premise of economic science. Hence the production of goods and wealth—by maximizing capital and achieving the growth rate to guarantee it—had been the imperative condition.

In modern economy, which has become an affluent one, the most urgent need is to establish guidelines to regulate development. These, however, are not intended to control the rate of increase (considered positive and ensured by a constantly self-propelling system) but, rather, to redistribute investment. The key is no longer that of redistributing existing wealth—the classical problem of equality—but of devolving the maximum disposable share of yielded income increase in order to convert the accumulation of capital to the public benefit. The purpose of this is to modify the living and working conditions of all members of the community (first of all, the depressed ones) in order to ensure security and a new social equilibrium. Social change then takes place within an economic structure which rejects traditional patterns. There is a new concept of wealth; it is no longer possible to rely on the myth of production of consumer goods. The growth concept, therefore, is radically changed.

Should a world still in search of itself and lacking the thrust of modern technology be confronted with the same dilemma as the modern affluent economy? The latter is struggling between the myth of production of consumer goods and the achievement of social equilibrium through the assumption of increasing social and civic responsibilities geared to individual and social capital incapable for the most part of being "quantified." Incentives and remuneration for work—which generate different behavior or reactions according to the mentality and expectations of individuals and groups—cannot be applied in underdeveloped areas on the basis of factors valid in other and, except for their "modernity," alien mental and economic contexts. Each element requires objective investigation, made in a spirit of cooperation in order to work out plans of action and to correct, if necessary, views based on other experiences.

The most recent studies seem to be leading slowly to a

thorough revision of the traditional concept of economic development, and are contributing to the definition of a new content. The economic growth-process, therefore, cannot be considered except as a process which transforms the whole society and which involves not only specific sectors but the society itself as a complex and historically formed organism. Economic change is thus a determining factor in promoting the growth-process. It is not, however, the only factor responsible for growth, since growth is an organic and orderly transformation of the economic and social structure, of cultural aims and attitudes, of administrative organization and juridical institutions. Social, cultural, juridical, and administrative changes must accompany economic change if this is to take hold and become effective in underdeveloped countries.

Obviously this does not exclude the even more fundamental theme: the goal to which society leads, or is led, and for which the adoption of adequate measures is politically justified and pursued. The effort to define that goal is an almost daily task in today's world, stimulated by an ever-expanding policy of planning and programming. It is already evident, however, that the experience of recent years has proved that the view of economic growth as organic expansion toward the ideal is the correct one. And this further lessens the time the Church has to find and fulfil its role in today's changing world.

Notes

[1] The present chapter is adapted from an article of the same author which appeared in *Concilium,* Vol. II, *The Church and the Liturgy* (Glen Rock, Paulist Press, 1965), pp. 161–180.

[2] B. F. Hoselitz, ed., *The Progress of Underdeveloped Areas* (Chicago, University of Chicago Press, 1952): "When people study the economic and technological growth they cannot understand the ultimate determinants of its process unless the line of demarcation between political economics and social anthropology is broken."

R. W. Goldsmith, *The Comparative Study of Economic Growth and Structure* (New York, National Bureau of Economic Research): "Economists and statisticians who work on the economic development problem must conclude that the ensemble of the measurable economic facts called by them 'growth' are closely bound with, and influenced by, the non-economic factor."

[3] C. Napoleoni, *Dizionario di Economia Politica* (Milan, 1956), p. 1556.

[4] Cf. R. Barre, *La Période dans l'Analyse Economique* (Paris, 1950), p. 15.

[5] A. Marshall, *Principles of Economics* (New York, Macmillan, 1922), p. 71.

[6] Cf. L. Robbins, *An Essay on the Nature and Significance of Economic Science* (London, St. Martins, 1935).

[7] Cf. H. Guitton, "Oscillation et Croissance", in *Economie Appliquée*, (Jan.–June 1954), pp. 178–206.

[8] Cf. P. A. Sorokin, *Society, Culture and Personality* (New York, Harper, 1947); Sorokin, *Social and Cultural Dynamics* (Boston, Sargent, 1957).

[9] Cf. "Le Contexte Socio-culturel et le Coût Social du Progrès", in *Le Tiers Monde* (Paris, 1956), pp. 289–303.

[10] P. Saraceno, *Iniziativa Privata e Azione Pubblica nei Piani di Sviluppo Economico* (Rome, 1959), pp. 13–14.

[11] G. Myrdal, *Teoria Economica e Paesi Sottosviluppati* (Milan, 1959), p. 129.

[12] G. Myrdal, *Une Economie Internationale* (Paris, 1958), pp. 225–226.

[13] Myrdal, *Teoria Economica e Paesi Sottosviluppati*, p. 21.

[14] Cf. Saraceno, *op. cit.*

SIX

The Church as Leaven in the World

THE CHURCH AND DEVELOPMENT

The Church's missionary history contains abundant evidence that preaching the kingdom of God has always been accompanied by the advancement of man's social, economic, and cultural well-being. The work of pioneer monks in Germanic Europe; the "reductions" of the Jesuits in Latin America; the systematization of indigenous languages; the hundreds of thousands of schools of every kind in Africa, Asia, Oceania; the religious orders formed to free slaves; the clinics, hospitals, dispensaries, agricultural cooperatives, and orphanages—all of these and more give witness to the innumerable efforts and enterprises for development carried out *ante litteram* through the centuries. In this sense the Church appears to be an important factor in the process of humanizing the world wherever it has been present.[1]

To be confirmed by more scientific analysis, however, this

judgment, positive in itself, must be set within fuller historical perspective. Opinions as to the most desirable and efficient methods of promoting development, especially in traditional societies, have fluctuated a great deal. They have undoubtedly been influenced by the various colonial experiences and the different significance given the terms and policies of "acculturation" and "integration," as well as by the scientific arguments to which these gave rise. The attitudes and functions of the activities undertaken by the Church, especially in the so-called "temporal" field, have therefore been subject to different interpretations. Before discussing them, it might be helpful to recall certain concepts presented in our earlier chapters.

Generally speaking, in the sociocultural context of development, ethical-religious motivations and the activities which they stimulate, can be analyzed as having a specific origin and influence within the various social systems and their related "zones of anomie." We can also acknowledge without difficulty that particular phenomena of social change, by revealing and accelerating the structural crises that overtake different societies, inevitably have an impact on religious motivations and attitudes and, therefore, on activities of religious inspiration and moral import.

In a still more general context, it may be said that the Church represents a system of values, many aspects of which are metahistorical. These values may seem and sometimes are dysfunctional, either with respect to the various societies or at some particular moment of their history. Certain aspects of this dynsfunctionalism are directly related to the "mystery" of the Church, while others result from the "divorce between the Church and the world." Whatever their nature, they are especially evident when social change leads to new structures and a preference for new values that first challenge and then create crisis in all types of social behavior, including those which are religiously motivated.

The immediate consequence of all this is that, by reason of the very factors of change, religious adherence demands a profound and specific maturity on the part of the individual and a type of social cohesion. This phenomenon necessitates a structural and cultural adaptation of considerable interest to the scholar and of primary importance for the "activities" of the Church.

We referred earlier to Thurling's analysis of progressive indifference toward the Church.[2] This indifference was produced by the presence and activities of secular institutions which were competing functional alternatives to ecclesistical institutions and activities, thus weakening the ecclesiastical mechanism of religious control. The Church defended itself against this threat to its existence in three principal ways: increasing through certain channels its influence on the external world, isolating itself in particular regions and areas, restructuring itself internally.

It is obvious from the Conciliar debates, and particularly from the discussions on the Constitution on the Church in the Modern World, that the Church cannot now react in either of the first two ways posited. Adaptation can be achieved only through internal restructuring. This is perhaps the clearest idea—and we hope the most valid "reform"—that emerged from Vatican Council II. In the same way, the Conciliar debates and statements on the nature of the Church lead to a revision of the Church's activities—a revision confirmed and validated by the evolution of historic reality.

Current trends affecting membership in various groups and engagement in various types of activity reflect the fact that interaction among social groups and knowledge of the techniques of production, communication, forecasting, and control of power exert a constant counter-influence, within the different groups, on acceptance of their own specific norms and values. The whole information complex, which introduces other standards and patterns, has expanded the area of direct psychological influence, affecting the deepest and most private motivations. Personal awareness of belonging is daily assailed by the dilemma posed by the encounter with different groups, roles, and institutions whose rhythms, modes of expression, and value scales seem to conflict. The confrontation breaks through narrow, local, or ghetto mentalities; it destroys their identification, their close or forced integration with the ethnic values of the community, gradually introducing ideas, motivations, and activities external to and transcending the frontiers of the traditional religious microstructures, whether of church or sect.

Thus, while the various basic institutions become increasingly specialized, secularized, and autonomous, the religious institution—no longer the axis of the local community—recovers its role as the inspirer of universalism and of ultimate ends. Its activities, as a consequence, are intrinsically purified by the very course of history. And, far from disappearing, the relation

between the religious institution and development is strengthened, not so much in the eschatological perspective as in the
historic modalities in which this is expressed. That this is not
a hazardous conclusion is evident from an analysis of the last
fifty years of missionary history.

It was already evident in the second half of the 19th century
that the accomplishments of the educational and health activities of the Christian missions had contributed to increased
production for the world market. While governments were
making substantial contributions to stimulate economic development, many missions sought to be a positive force in
furthering this development, and they succeeded. When world
markets became shaky and prices fell, the value of government
efforts, and consequently of the mission contribution, gradually
changed.

In the first decade of the 20th century, the churches and
their missions began to look on the rapid economic development with a critical eye. Living and social conditions for
mine and farm workers, and even more for the rootless
groups of workers in industrialized cities, were becoming un-
bearable. From 1920–1940 the churches concentrated their
attention on social rather than economic problems, principally
in urban and industrial centers. Depending on the region and
the urgency of the problems, the attitude of the churches grew
further apart from the policies and financing of the governments. At the risk of oversimplification, it might be said that
the churches accepted commercial and industrial enterprises as
necessary for the body and the development of material life,
but dangerous for the soul and spiritual life. For their part

the governments, often officially, considered the missions of real benefit only to the extent that the latter did not oppose their interests or meddle in government affairs.

All of this could have led inevitably to a real, even if unspectacular, break between the missions on one hand and development policies on the other. But this same period saw a growing desire for a clearer understanding and more complete evaluation of the phenomenon of development. From the end of World War II onward development activity constituted a series of tests for both the concept of development to be kept in mind and the "strategy" to be adopted. The need for industrialization and economic infrastructures increased, and governments assumed the dominant role in economic planning and decisions regarding sectors of investment.

In this overall climate the missions were compelled to keep up with events, but they lacked the means and authority to make a positive contribution. With the increasingly rapid growth of urban centers, however, they concentrated on social work, engaging in a kind of "industrial evangelism." But in the fields of communication, transportation, energy, capital investment, there was little they could do.

In addition, international agencies of economic development —the United Nations programs, the World Bank, bilateral agreements and investments—entered the framework of national policy, but these elude the sphere of the competence and authority of religious institutions. Since development was considered primarily economic, the missions necessarily were observers rather than participants.

On the other hand, a vast field of activity was opening up

for missions with the emergence of new nations. The churches, their missions, and the Christians of both the developed and the developing countries were faced with a new responsibility; confrontation with the nationalist, social, and economic forces of the new nations could no longer be avoided or ignored.

From 1950–1960, and even more in the decade of the sixties, attention has been directed increasingly to the deficiencies in social infrastructures. We noted above the increased interest in the social and cultural changes which condition economic development. Education, sanitation and health services, social structures, basic attitudes and mentalities, began to be evaluated for their positive or negative influence on social and economic progress. In a relatively short time the social scientists came up with studies on the obstacles to rapid, balanced development, which are basic to any treatment of the subject. At this point the churches and missionary movements immediately caught an appeal which was much more familiar to them. The ancient wisdom of the adage that "man is body and soul and cannot be considered apart from his society" was being confirmed on every side. This meant active participation in the global process by all the churches and all religions, which therefore had to redefine their "mission."

In Africa and Asia especially, the process of decolonization was giving rise to a new organization of society and, consequently, creating a new dimension for the role of religion. Missionary effort, which began under colonial administrations and was often encouraged and supported by the latter, now needed new identification, new guarantees, and new methods. In addition to the changed situations created by newly independent governments, there was the rebirth of many strong and widespread non-Christian movements which pushed Christians back into a minority position. The search for a new role in temporal activity in relation to national and social development thus became urgent.

In Latin America, where the Catholic Church held the majority position while the Protestant denominations formed a small minority, different historic circumstances led to the same kind of crisis. During the 19th century, with the exception of one or two countries, the relations between Church and State had been very strained and little attention had been given to social and economic problems. The struggle for education, especially at the secondary level, had become the most acute problem. Many reactions of the Catholic Church in Latin-American countries were motivated by a kind of "ideal" —to restore the order of things that existed before the advent of the contemporary, antagonistic society. This situation, however, has changed radically in the last fifteen years. Although there is still a strong conservative element in the Catholic Church, many of its positions promote basic social reform to speed up development; and many of the larger Protestant groups have taken the same positions. In addition to declarations of principle and statements of position, a great number of initiatives have been undertaken to assist social reform and economic development, beginning with local efforts to organize resources or grass-roots movements—e.g., radio-schools, fundamental education, cooperatives, trade unions, political parties drawing their inspiration from Christian social teaching.

In Latin America, as in Asia and Africa, the problem is the same: the new temporal role in relation to social and national development. The Church, as a religious community which gives witness to Christ in the world, is called upon to declare itself in the debate on the final ends historically pursuable by mankind in the process of development and on the use of adequate means to ensure total participation in the existential global movement, so that there will be no repetition of the dichotomy between temporal and eternal destiny, temporal and spiritual activity, between the Church and the world. The whole world expects the Church to pronounce itself, both in the analysis of its serving role and the evaluation of its recent historical experience, on the subject of development. This pronouncement would express to the whole world the church's awareness that humanity is struggling and progressing toward better stages of life and action. The Church, as leaven in the world, cannot fail to be aware of the present ferment in mankind, with all its dangers and its hopes, precisely because the Church cannot be separated from the world, precisely because the Church is on pilgrimage toward the fullness of the Parousia —and, therefore, the one historical reality in this world.

The Church's position with respect to development, if it is to be a vital one, must begin with a phenomenology of the modern world. This does not require an exhaustive and itemized cataloging of all the elements and tensions of contemporary societies, but it is essential to keep in mind those which are most significant and most operative within the historical context; for, more than anything else, it is the mean-

ing of tomorrow's history in today's present that is of interest
to the Church of Christ.

This meaning finds expression in signs which gradually
bring to the surface of the collective religious consciousness
new forms of the one divine call to build sacred history.
Mentioned briefly here are a few of these signs which seem
particularly to call for the Church's responsibility in relation
to development.

Intrinsic Acceleration of History

With man's increased dominion over nature, through multiple
forms of cooperation and social interdependence, and with
the triumph of a positive politico-social attitude toward planning, there has come a kind of revelation. Modern man is
aware that there is for every individual the possibility of complete fulfillment of his potentialities within his life span. All
this has come about within a few years and in "periods of
awareness" previously unknown. As a result of this accelerated
collective awareness, which produces and accompanies the
acceleration of history (i.e., the sequence of human acts), the
gamut of roles and possibilities for action open to every individual is extended immeasurably, and so too is the possibility of concrete freedom for every human being.

This acceleration is the result of a cumulative process
brought about by technical progress which has reduced
distances and considerably enlarged the ambit of communications. For the first time in history, the multiplicity of varying

social situations is superseded by actual international inter-dependence. There is instant generalization of new patterns and modes of behavior, as well as knowledge of the limits to which a potential mass-consumption civilization can extend.

For contemporary societies the phenomenon of acceleration is concretized in the possibility of foreseeing the satisfaction of social needs through the technology, planning, and high degree of social organization at their disposal. It is evident, however, that this phenomenon, like every human effort, can have ambiguous results. For example, there is the danger of failing to go beyond the confines of the mass-consumption culture, of leaving outside the circle of well-being those who have not had the time or resources to reach it, of stifling at the nerve center of a given social situation the very process of awareness that gives a community the sense of playing a part in its own history and that of the world.

Socialization

The world is moving steadily toward greater socialization, that is, toward increasingly complex forms of social integration and community life. Socialization is a term used to stress, in the increasing complexity of human relations, the aspect of unity—both psychological and institutional, individual and collective.[3] The introduction and expansion of the techniques of production and communication surpass the dimensions and objectives of individuals and of single societies and stimulate them toward increasingly conscious and coordinated forms of community and association. Socialization is, therefore, a historic, global, unitary process. The achievements of technology have made men increasingly interdependent; and conscious of this, they find in society, viewed in universal terms, the complex of institutions in which and through which it is possible to discover and pursue a fundamental and ultimate unity. They understand the need for means of identification and guarantees which allow association with greater security and lead to the more rapid and equal attainment of individual and collective objectives.

Awareness of socialization is penetrating in varying degree all manifestations of contemporary life and conditioning the conduct of society. It is unnecessary, therefore, to belabor the obvious importance of this twentieth-century characteristic. It is enough to note the fundamental pressure it is creating for redefining the dynamics of power and authority, for breaking through nationalistic barriers, and for establishing new obligatory principles for world solidarity and community. All this is clearly evidenced in the new types of agreement being contracted and the degree of international awareness that is striving to eliminate violence, discrimination, and hunger.

Socialization enriches the sum of social responsibilities and duties. Just as earlier centuries succeeded in abolishing slavery, in promoting recognition of the dignity of women, in humanizing working conditions to some extent, so today it can be said that oppression and violence, in relation to minority groups within a given national society, are no longer tolerable.

Rationalization

The progress of civilization was characterized for the last century by the control of physical energy which followed the Industrial Revolution. Today this control is being extended to the entire organization of social life through the widespread acceptance of rationalization as a social process. This means the objectification of the group attitudes involved in weighing the reasons for specific actions against a detailed scrutiny of their alternatives and of the integration necessary in view of their interrelationships and consequences. Through rationalization, as much risk as possible is eliminated in both individual and group actions, for these are reduced to their logical content in full knowledge of their social results and further productivity.

This phenomenon, which is now widely influencing social practice, is largely responsible for the growing trend toward planning. Planning adds a new dimension to the problem of government in contemporary society. It may be defined as the State's taking over all economic projection and forecasting and determining in what sectors entities "inferior" to the State should invest. The trend toward planning—as an expression of the rationalization phenomenon—is evident in the compulsory organization of various activities with a socioeconomic import, such as migration movements, population control, national savings, increased manpower training in special skills, economic controls, according to a strict scale of priority needs.

While it is one of the most profound manifestations of

man's control over his social environment, rationalization nevertheless places an extraordinary precision instrument for progress at the mercy of a determining mechanism of authority and social conditioning. Thus it adds another serious dimension to the contemporary dynamics of power. Rationalization can become a tool for domination as well as for service. It produces a new kind of social sovereignty, that of the "technocrats," whose management of social authority goes much deeper and is much more complex than that exercised by the old bureaucratic-military bloc.

As man is placed increasingly at the mercy of man in the actual development process, these "signs of the times" urge upon everyone the responsibility to be mindful of all that is "human." They demand awareness of the complicated web of augmented powers which may operate for the benefit of man, *or* against him, and which are the source of the great contemporary tensions.

The Church's task is to plumb in depth the significance of all these signs, which become part of sacred history as living opportunities offered by God so that man may respond to the fundamental call of his nature, the innermost thrust of his being. But an understanding of the "signs of the times" cannot and must not be the charismatic privilege of only a few of her children. It is coessential with the Church's prophetic function as a community, the People of God on the march. The Church's response to the global phenomenon of development, therefore, must come from the whole Church, involving the integral responsibility of each and all its members according to the particular virtues and gifts bestowed by the Holy Spirit.

INTERNAL REFORM

In dealing with the changes that arise and that we must accept and further in the historical process in which we are living, we must stress two fundamental principles, too often forgotten or wrongly invoked in all discussions on the Church.

As a cultural system and as a social system, the Church is a temporary instrument with respect to the human person. It is the human person—whether as an individual or as a member of the groups in which he is born, develops, and acts— that is the final object of the Church's action. There is no justification for any action on the part of the Church, for any provision, rite, advancement, except as it concerns the real, living human person. It is not enough to say that the Church safeguards the magisterium which preserves and confirms the best definition of the human person. The entire clarification action of the magisterium is for the human person. Its chief purpose is not to define him; it is to enable this real, living person—each one of us—to find, through his conscience and his free decisions, his personal response to the call of God.

Intimately connected with this is the fact that the Church is the People of God on pilgrimage toward the fulfillment of its destiny. Social needs, divine guarantees in the exercise of the magisterium, and pastoral functions must not obscure the fundamental fact that the Church is all Christians—not just bishops, priests, and members of religious orders. Whatever the function or rank in the Church, it has a definite social purpose; even the sacrament of Holy Orders is a permanent assignment to the *service of a community,* which lives, reacts, and develops according to its own rhythms and in response to the new exigencies continually arising.

These principles are essential to the Church and furnish the key to whatever the dialectic convergence of the changes in the Church and the world may suggest by way of reform. It is precisely this assignment to the service of man, the whole man and every man, which can and must provide the lever to pry loose the obstacles which have piled up in the intricate vicissitudes of human life, even within the Church, and which lie firmly embedded in the dust of centuries.

Ecclesiastical Structure

The changes in attitude and mentality necessary for a contemporary interpretation of the Church's basic functions require new mechanisms throughout the entire ecclesiastical structure, whether at the center or at the periphery.

In the first place, a clear distinction must be made between directive organs and those for research, between organs for collegial decisions and administrative organs. The definition of episcopal collegiality is only one stage in this process of clarification. It has restored responsibility to and defined the field of action for bishops, whether acting singly or acting conjointly in national or continental "colleges"; but many other problems remain unsolved. Still to be defined are the relationship between these episcopal colleges and the Roman

Curia, the role of the senate of bishops in relation to the Pope and as the voice of the entire episcopate, the relationship between bishops' conferences and collegiality. While it is true that many controversial points came to the surface during the Conciliar debates and that several of the aforementioned questions urgently require adequate answers, it is equally true that genuine reform can be achieved only by using some of the principles borrowed from other sciences. There are techniques for more effective coordination of functions and offices which could very well be used in adapting collegial powers to the principles of subsidiarity and decentralization in keeping with standards for efficiency and function.

The problem is both juridical and technical. It is necessary to move from the precise definition of duties and competencies to very simple and effective program descriptions for the various bodies. One of the great ambiguities which still bedevils certain circles is the confusion between these two phases. Closely related to this is the serious confusion among the various internal levels of the papal function. It is well-known that the latter includes the Bishop of Rome, the Patriarch of the West and the Latin world, and the Successor of St. Peter with the divine right of primacy. This has led to great confusion and ambiguity, the persistence of which has been due mainly to the timidity and excessive respect which, in servile minds, have stifled the sense of duty and responsibility. No one will deny that one of the expressions most fatal to the development of a mature conscience is the oft-repeated phrase—heard even in the Council—"this is the thinking at the top . . . ," reflecting almost a fear of expressing

one's own views or of stating things and men as they are. The
anonymity of the Curia has proved in the course of time to be
one of the subtlest means of weakening the power of the
Christian conscience. Then there is the equally mischievous
confusion between investigative procedures, administrative procedures, and *foro interno* procedures in which it is impossible
to know the extent of a right because of a custom that is treated
as law. There is confusion about the authority an individual
has to conduct inquiries outside his own field of competence,
confusion over the right to levy financial contributions. It is
in these areas especially that application of the principles of
organizational science would save energy and funds, for there
is much wastage of both. With the end of the Council, which
concentrated on the pastoral function, the renewal already
in the air has encountered an atmosphere ready for adaptation
to new structures. There are new fields of specialization, and
some traditional structures have either been rendered obsolete
by the course of history or have lost their importance. Decentralization, the need for which is recognized at all levels
even outside the Church, calls for new competencies and new
associative and voluntary organisms, to which the law will
give formal recognition without presuming to fix their character or field of action. The principle of subsidiarity will never
be valid except in a system in which the Council statements
on religious liberty can be operative. In this connection there
is a whole series of procedures which must be inspired by
these declarations, for it has not been the concept of punishment so much as the procedures used, with no legal provision
for appeal, which too often violated inalienable rights. Ob-

viously it is very difficult to temper the odium of penalty, even for the "good of the sinner," with the safeguard of freedom. But this would be precisely the most valued effort the new code of Canon Law could undertake.

The changes concerning ecclesiastical offices and benefices should be considered along these same lines. The connection between the two has been nonexistent for some time; in actual practice, however, it is possible to accumulate them, and there are also somewhat unjust impediments to obtaining them. Holding to the principle of incardination, thus affiliating the clergy with a particular diocese, is a serious obstacle to the mobility of ecclesiastical personnel—even though, in the absence of other guarantees, it offers the one secure basis for recognition and maintenance. The principal of incardination should at least be broadened to allow a redistribution of clergy that will be more responsive to the needs of the People of God and of individual vocations rather than to diocesan limits, which are often narrow and inadequate. This principle, along with that of assigning offices and related benefices through competition, should be readapted to the pastoral whole; its administration should be organized for efficiency and economy, and ultimately finalized according to budgets worked out by the whole local community.

Along with a reform of procedures, greater mobility for personnel, and more careful and efficient administration, a new juridical structure for the organs of coordination should be envisaged. Decentralization and subsidiarity call for stable and flexible structures for communication, liaison, and co-ordination. There can be no effective reform without direction and a permanent structure to ensure quick communication and local response. There has been too little use in the Church of the principle of feedback, so that there is a constant effort to correct, integrate, or confirm the reactions to decisions. Internal dialogue among all the members must be part of the entire daily routine, and certain bottlenecks should be eliminated. Coordination permits the maximum use of energies to the correct degree and prevents duplication and wasteful use of means and energy.

The crisis in traditional microstructures in relation to religious adherence has already been discussed in earlier parts of this work.[4] This crisis not only makes integration difficult for the individual and involves finding a new type of bond for belonging, which must be defined and to which the believer must be educated, but it also requires revision of the pastoral structures on the basis of new sociogeographic units. As Father Pin observes,

In a traditional society each local community constitutes a relatively complete and independent unity, within which most problems can be resolved. In addition, the independent work of small units, of educational groups, even of individuals, corresponds to the dimensions of the problems. The task of the central organisms of the State or of the Church is to arbitrate—to choose—among the requests for men and resources which come from the different communities. The strategy is one of distribution. Once this is worked out, the decision as to what should be done can easily be left to the good judgment of the local group. In a specialized and "associational" society, problems take on a world, continental, or at least national dimension. It is often in the great international or national capitals that the lot of local communities is decided. The main ideological movements are worldwide. Permanent economic, political, and cultural relations are interwoven among nations. In generalized interdependence, isolated action at the local community level becomes obsolete . . . the world bodies, the continental or national organisms are more important for the local communities than local organisms. Therefore, decisions, to avoid the twofold risk of central authoritarianism and local inefficiency, must be "collegial," that is, they must be taken jointly by all the community leaders assembled together. . . . Horizontal cooperation is all the more necessary the more specialized, and therefore the more complementary, the individuals or organizations in the same area.[5]

The pastoral consequences of these observations are quite evident. It is essential to develop a real series of governing bodies, communities, commissions, each charged with specific problems and with the task of gathering the necessary materials and formulating decisions. They should not be merely advisory bodies, but should share the responsibility involved; for most of today's problems are not only beyond a single superior's capacity to devote the necessary study to them but also go beyond his individual responsibility. The specific details of this network of centers for research, work, and action in the Church will have to be worked out on the basis of experience. In such a network every individual should feel protected from sterile evasions, and through it the traditional local quarrels, those forms of Catholic provincialism, could be abolished. It is clear by now that the action of a single in-

dividual has an importance in the great work of salvation;
but today it is group action and community value that count,
and the Church has to create new structures that will enable
new motivations to find suitable channels of expression and
of effectiveness in the world.

Reform of basic structures is not enough unless it brings
with it reform of relational structures. A few reflections on
group life drawn from social psychology may be helpful
here. The defense structure must give way to a preventive one
that will obviate inadequacies and nonadaptation. In other
words, instead of being based on the concept of assistance
(and punishment for the delinquent), the structure should
be such as to stimulate energies, vitalize community spirit,
and develop fraternal solidarity. This means the existence, or
at least the juridical possibility of existence, of services and
exchanges on matters with which all members of the Church
are involved by the simple fact of their living in the world,
and on the subjective opinions each member forms regarding
these matters. The aid structure is paternalistic, even in the
picture it presents of a given situation and in the individual
reactions it creates. *A priori*, on the basis of the normative
principles which seek to establish its legitimacy, it takes the
place of positive research—which is often long, painful, and
contradictory but which demonstrates that the statement of objective fact makes no sense unless it is related to the emotions
that make it lived reality to individuals and groups. Consequently, a preventive and stimulative structure, a true instrumental service for the individual person and for all

persons, must allow for the presence and action of natural leaders, who, with their different attitudes and tendencies, can and should be incorporated into the structure itself. Up to the present time leaders have been chosen as instruments within a defensive paternalistic framework in which they were considered to be spiritual "minors," due in large measure to the sacral concept of power and authority.

This change of structure directly involves the concept of the Church's internal law. It does not challenge the hierarchical structure as much as it challenges the elaboration, interpretation, and application of the Church's concept of the positive norm. The principles for this change are already laid down in Canon Law, but it is easy to see how a general change of attitude in the Church—with, for example, the Declaration on Religious Freedom—necessarily leads to revision of certain procedures bearing on the freedom of the believer, the system of concordats, mixed marriages, choice of schools, etc. It requires, therefore, a broad revision of relational structures which permit challenge and discussion.

Within this broader context, the reform of the Curia is only a first step, of great importance but not guaranteeing that the whole body of ecclesiastical structures will change overnight. There will be the inevitable periods of trial and error, and it is to be hoped that sufficient time will be allowed for a kind of creative chaos, with control only over basic intentions and a check only on what are genuine and specific aberrations. The imperative of reform is ever to put at man's disposal an area in which he feels completely free to follow his vocation in communion with his brothers and with the prospect of attaining results that will gladden his being as a Christian.

In conclusion, we should mention the reforms already underway with respect to the official relations of the Church, as a socioreligious body, not only with nation-States but also with the communities of other Christians, non-Christians, and nonbelievers. In the atmosphere of the Council, new horizons were opened up for dialogue and for life in common with these brothers. The Church will have to think about creating continuing structures for dialogue which are not confined to secretariats at the center of Christianity. Here, too, it would be well to leave the doors open and to listen to the voices of free and generous spirits, to draw from the experience of other groups and from future developments the elements that will make for a true, stable dialogue structure at every level.

Ecclesiastical Culture

Change in the ecclesiastical structure cannot be achieved—or be truly effective—without change in the ecclesiastical culture.

To touch on this subject is to risk being charged with integralism or modernism, for the ambiguities begin to appear only in comparison with the general culture. Nevertheless, the following observations are the logical consequence of the preceding chapters, and they are an integral part of any discussion geared to arriving at a true *aggiornamento* without losing contact with the reality of living tradition.

In the training of clergy, what is necessary above all is a

positive method. This has been used only in a few subjects taught in seminaries, often because of the very nature of their content. By a positive method for all ecclesiastical learning, we mean the attitude of evaluating and experiencing culture in its historicist and pluralistic dimensions. The immutability of dogma, the certainty of the privilege of possessing a truth consecrated in precise concepts, the fact that it derives from a deposit that must be preserved—all this has for a long time hindered the acceptance of the sense of history in passing on the teaching.

Only recently has it been possible to disentangle historical from dogmatic tradition; only recently have the disciplines dealing with actions (moral and pastoral theology, Canon Law, etc.) included the excursus on the relative evolution they have undergone in the course of time; only recently has the use of literary forms been admissible in the interpretation of the Bible; and only since the beginning of this century has it been possible to distinguish between speculative and positive theology. It is clear that the usual documentation, the search for proof, and the structure of argumentation are not the exclusive patrimony of authority—even though authority is needed in the teaching of dogma to authenticate its premises or the partial conclusions from which it starts and at which it arrives.

In the run-of-the-mill seminary training, there is an *a priori* mentality, for which everything is already neatly classified and resolved, which considers any opposition of the individual conscience to the overwhelming proof of authority and majority opinion the mere child of foolish fancy, and which does not accept the alternative of error and the erring except in terms of condemnation. This *a priori* character excludes, therefore, something that is a positive datum of the modern world, namely, the many different anthropological, psychological, and sociological visions, which need only to be integrated toward a final end by religion. Religion alone can guarantee their integration, but only by accepting their existence and spheres of autonomy.

It will be said that ecclesiastical culture has always absorbed the various types of new knowledge which man has progressively acquired in the course of time. But no one has had the courage to state that the use of this knowledge has been instrumental only and that religious judgment—or better, classification in definite and convenient typologies—has served to guarantee that the new subject matter could be used for the "holy cause" without a true appreciation of its content or of the individual or group research that produced it. An example of this harmful tendency, which has kept many sincere persons from joining or even sympathizing with the Church, has been the misguided extension of these procedures to all of so-called "Catholic culture." This created watertight compartments in "Catholic thought" and in social ambiences and strata, thus preventing the natural osmosis of various experiences in knowledge. Through zeal for religious unity, it smothered the pronounced differences between the various fields of specialization, which require intellectual breathing space and fields for experimental application rather than membership cards. The integralist mentality unfortunately is still a feature of ecclesiastical culture. One of the most immediate consequences of this has been loss of status in the broader complex of human knowledge, accompanied by diminution of religious knowledge and of the role played by the religious institution.

Acceptance of the positive method means engaging in dialogue, watching the world in order to grasp the "signs of the times" and to understand the problems and needs of men and the natural call to religion which reveals itself in constantly changing ways. It involves radical reform of the Church's research and training institutes, the creation of a new type of university, and the organization of a cultural "mission." In the educational field the modern world is attracted by the polytechnic, the symbol of scientific humanism. Ecclesiastical culture must have at its disposal a higher type of training which, in the field of religious integration, is the equivalent of the natural and social sciences. Educational institutions should be open to everyone, because all Christians have a right to advanced training, and they should afford a meeting place for the best minds and best men of action. Social science experts and theologians should find therein the ideal place and climate for debate and the most exacting student audience.

The Council, by bringing together bishops and experts in the various commissions, started a process of cultural osmosis for which a continuing structure will have to be created in the Church and in the dialogue with other religions. This means the end of police-like controls, odious prejudices, and *nihil obstats* in discussion and debates. It means opening the door to every man of good will, accepting every honest contribution from whatever person it comes. The certain possession of the fullness of truth should not fear encounter with doubt, for faith is quite different from learning and culture. Logically, this attitude of mind supposes greater maturity than that to which "traditional" training has accustomed us. A protective system of education cannot last today. There is a constant, almost systematic invasion by the external world into every sector of the individual's life. Criticism is as much a part of the modern climate as the understanding of relativity. The categories of traditional ecclesiastical learning are still too rigid; they need to be critically reviewed and pruned of all unjustified absolutism. Above all, it is necessary to distinguish learning *per se* from what is a norm of faith, elaboration of concepts related to given moments of history and specific sociocultural milieus from dogmatic pronouncement. The theological pluralism whose fruitfulness was at the basis of Conciliar debates cannot be stifled by a false uniformity. Such pluralism enriches the religious patrimony and does not weaken obedience where mature men are concerned. The stewardship of the sacred deposit of truth must conform to the evangelical criterion of disseminating *nova et vetera* and cannot confine itself to guarding a hidden treasure.

It is in this framework that the problem of spreading the Christian message is to be considered. Modern means of communication have often been used in the service of the Word. But the time has come to think of true pastoral action in the cultural field—especially in committed cultures—based on open dialogue with all contemporary currents. Any action in this field must be a broad encounter with all the various currents, involving the responsibility of the whole Church. It must be approached with an attitude quite different from that which, in the society of its own time, justified the Tridentine catechism. In today's world literacy is more wide-spread and the average cultural level much higher. Sacral and superstitious encrustations must be cut away for all the people; the process cannot be confined to elites or special coteries, thereby perpetuating a double Christianity. The best reforms require both courage and adjustment and have to be worked out by experts if they are to have an impact on popular customs and practices. A basic religious culture in today's world cannot begin—or end—with memorizing a penny catechism written for other mentalities; this contains too many obscurities that need clarification, too many norms that are no longer a guide for conduct, too many conflicting values, too many useless doubts.

Reform of ecclesiastical culture means taking into account this whole series of problems, resolving them with clarity, and putting today's Christians at ease in the cultural debate. This is the point of friction and perhaps the most dramatic aspect of the present period through which the Church is passing, for it demands a concentration of men and means, the use of adequate measures, and the complete assumption of respon-sibility. Transition is very difficult in a living organism like the Church in which charisms, the prophetic element, and the hierarchical structure are matters of faith. Control becomes most difficult and, at the same time, most necessary. Here, as for other aspects of the hierarchical structure, it would be well to adopt some principles of the management theory, so that control would be only an element in the information and formation process, not an activity in itself. In addition, the control process would be directed toward analyzing the effects of and reactions to the informative and formative action rather than hindering or giving compulsory direction to the action itself. Since the Declaration on Religious Freedom and the Constitution on the Church, this viewpoint should need no further discussion.

The phases through which the whole social body, at various levels, will respond to decisions are quite evident. In the first place, there is the basic information stage, properly so called, through which knowledge of the situations in which pastoral action is to be carried on is acquired and set forth with relevant data. Secondly, there is the planning process, which defines possible courses of action (including "passivity" and the "tendency to follow the traditional course") along with their respective costs and effects. Thirdly, there is the process of evaluation, in which alternatives are chosen and norms established for the executive organs. And finally, there is the control process which establishes subsystems of communication and information to determine the effects of the decisions.

In the ecclesiastical culture—and in the decision-making organs both at the center and in the field—these various phases have often been confused or unconnected. As a consequence, control has gradually invaded the whole information and formation field. When the chief preoccupation is one of prevention, especially in a closed society like that assailed from within by the Reformation, recourse to stricter control might seem the most effective method. The institution of the Congregation of the Holy Office, and later the Index of forbidden books, should be viewed in this context. But today the speed and technical efficiency with which information is communicated, the dissemination of news on a world scale together with its anonymous character, the Church's minority position in an open society in which more or less everyone has access to the products of culture, the existence of a real cultural industry in competition with or in opposition to official organs of the word and of language—all these render traditional control impossible, obsolete, and at times uselessly ridiculous. In addition, the modern mind is resistant to paternalistic or authoritarian positions. The spirit of criticism leads to a desire to taste the cultural products for oneself, with confidence, rightly or wrongly, in the maturity of one's own judgment.

The task of the ecclesiastical culture is to ensure for the Church the entire ambit of information, and this can be achieved only to the extent that dialogue and the techniques of communication become social custom for all members of the Church. This is no more than a response to the exigencies of modern life. The wheelbase of this *aggiornamento* of ecclesiastical culture could be the establishment, at the center and in the field, of study and research centers in statistics, sociology, anthropology, and especially interdisciplinary centers with committees of theologians and pastoral experts. In such a framework there would be opportunity for developing new types of specialization, including those related to information and documentation. Public opinion in the Church could thus be a process of awareness and not the expression

of extemporaneous expedients; it could provide that climate
of responsible freedom in which everyone, being at ease, would
be able to give his best for the common good of all.

PASTORAL ACTION

Changes in ecclesiastical structure and culture inevitably involve changes in pastoral activity, which has to be organic
and community-minded. Pastoral action must be characterized
by an understanding of the collective aspects of modern life.
It must re-present the religious values of the community in
today's terms. It must be sensitive to the importance of the
adult personality, keeping in mind the values of the psychology of personality, and renewing the appeal, in freedom, to
the generous spirit of man in search of his identity. Although
these are conclusions which can be drawn from the preceding
pages, it would be well to consider further some of their more
evident aspects which have already stimulated new currents
of thought and action, both before and after the Council.

Modern life is characterized above all by the phenomenon
of vast dimensions. In fact, in our present-day industrial
society, the great dimensions of its socioeconomic structures—
their origins, functions, and action—are almost tangible.
Boulard has repeatedly stressed the importance of the collective aspect of the pastoral problem which derives from this
phenomenon. Man today is increasingly conditioned by the
dimensions of his social environment and by realities that are
not individual in nature. It would be ridiculous to persist in
an individualistic view of pastoral action, which—although

its aim is indeed the salvation of individual persons—is of necessity embodied in the structures of the present world. It is precisely the incarnation of the Christian message which requires a collective and social manifestation connected with modern life; otherwise, there will be that perennial divorce between the public and private sectors which is too often a product of the view that religion is a personal and private matter. The Church—as the sacrament of salvation, the visible sign of Christ in the world, and therefore as the community of salvation—has been, and still is being, assailed by all the typical forms of life in a developed society. The Church has been, or certainly will be, purified and lightened of all social "compensatory" activities; it has been restored to its specific character as a religious institution. But this does not alter the fact that the Church must have a social physiognomy, which is community, the visible sign of Christ.

The period of crisis through which the Church is passing in the search for new forms of presence in the world has led to much discussion of the "crisis of religion." It has been theorized that religion will no longer have a dynamic social role, for individuals or for groups, and will withdraw or confine itself to the unconscious levels of the modern spirit. This theory is reinforced, to some degree, by the critical situation of urban parishes caught in a number of problems concerning their administrative-territorial position, the organization of liturgical services, and their cellular structure in relation to the larger diocesan or national whole. This means that traditional religious microstructures cannot exist by themselves and make their presence and social influence felt in the broad dimensions of modern society. It is evident, therefore, that new modalities must be found for pastoral action, a new type of relationship between its traditional and irreplaceable functions and the mechanisms through which it can be effective in the present-day world. The broad dimensions of modern society cannot be affected from within the confines of small, quasi-autonomous communities that are turned in upon themselves. What is needed is coordination of different forces and groups, whose social pressure is much greater than that of the traditional parochial communities and is leavened by a much greater infusion of voluntarism. In a quantitative sense, pastoral action must match these greater dimensions through geographical extension, broadening its specialized services to cover whole urban or regional areas. Qualitatively, it must be sufficiently aware of and tuned to the mutability and variety of milieus and mentalities. On the organizational level, there must be better distribution of personnel and financial resources, more efficient training centers. Pastoral action will be truly effective only when it is set within the framework of the broader "whole" and coordinated on the diocesan and interdiocesan levels or for socially and religiously homogeneous areas. It is obvious that the creation of the necessary structures requires the aid of the scientific disciplines whose clear, fruitful cooperation was sought by the Council.

We cannot assume, however, that this type of *aggiornamento* alone will be either sufficient or effective. An enormous vacuum—worse than the one we are trying to fill—would be created if this pastoral effort were viewed only in organizational terms and not connected with the most vital and appealing sectors of theological renewal: Scripture and liturgy. Precisely in relation to the signs of the times which demand adaptation to society's broad dimensions, pastoral action will have to stress the community values of religion, which only the widespread reading of the Word of God and participation in the liturgy can make clear for Christians and for the whole world. One should, in fact, mistrust those who place themselves in the forefront of pastoral renewal without this theological concern. The fruitful interaction between theology and experience will provide the Christian community with new structures of vital force, representational strength, and spiritual pressure in today's world.

This leads us immediately to another set of phenomena that cannot fail to influence the revision of pastoral action. These are the phenomena related to socialization, namely, the movement toward social unity through the lively and growing complexity of all the groups, organs, and functions which characterize it. Now this movement lacks the thrust of an ideal, a compelling and satisfying motivation. It is a paradox of modern society that while men are being increasingly impelled toward forms of association, they do not feel compelled by ideal motives from within. They are pushed along by a new form of social necessity in a quasi-automatic process. The liberalization of society is thus accompanied by a kind of disinterestedness and detachment that create a no-man's-land at the very heart of social life and a sense of emptiness in the daily compulsory interweaving of social relationships.

The lack of an ideal thrust explains the number of in-

termediate organisms and the crisis that exists today in all
types of belonging—in political parties, trade unions, churches,
etc. The problem here for pastoral action is to make the religious experience of the individual and the group coincide
with the need for ideal motivation. This means revitalizing
the associative spirit through rediscovery of the values of
solidarity and equality inherent in the religion of love. Historically, the Church has performed a most important function
in society. Through its capacity for change and the actual
changes it has undergone, the Church has encouraged—in a
variety of ways and through a broad scope of different
activities—an open-ended gamut of associations based, not on
some ephemeral political or civic situation of the moment,
but on values capable of providing valid motives for action
even in the most contradictory circumstances. Take, for
example, the Church in the transitional period of the Dark
Ages or in the complex structure of the Middle Ages, with
its intricate network—so congenial to the spirit of the times—
of orders, congregations, guilds, confraternities, associations,
etc. While the Western nation-State did away with corporative
structures only in the post-revolutionary free-trade period and
now seems to be going back to them in other ways (though
with different intent and juridical orientation), the Church
has lagged behind in this area due to its preoccupation with
defense against attacks from without and the invasion from
within of a certain tendency to individualistic piety. The
Church, therefore, emerged with an appeal to the laity which
produced the various so-called Catholic Action movements.
These movements, however, were too closely allied with the

need for defense and with a concept of the laity's role as an instrument of the direct authority which the hierarchy felt was being rejected by a secularized world. The climate today is quite different. There is a blossoming of groups which— whether composed of clergy or lay persons—have found in the living sources of Christianity and the associative tradition that had never disappeared new opportunities for presence and action. It is not merely assistance to these groups that should be the object of pastoral action today so much as providing the ideal inspiration for social action on the part of any existing organism in our pluralistic society, thus further- ing the presence of Christians—as Christians—in the building of man's world.

F. Balbo rightly observes:

The laity wavers between acting like priests and acting like non- Christians. Yet the Church should become evident to non-Christians through the laity and to the laymen themselves through their re- ciprocal witness rather than through the priests. The priests, the hierarchy, are the most internal feature of Christianity and the least communicable to others. The period we are in today is the reverse of that in which Christianity was first spread abroad by the Apostles. The successors of the Apostles cannot re-announce the Gospel message except through the witness of the Christian laity. This witness, as such, is not holiness . . . but the concrete evidence that by being Christian they are men, and by being Chris- tian they realize their humanity. . . . Christians must act, like all men, for the generation and regeneration of man and for the at- tainment of human community; only for this reason do they defend the rights of the Church and work for her progress. In acting for the generation of man, Christians will manifest their identity by refusing to accept superficial or mechanistic approaches or solutions, by rejecting Machiavellianisms, by their capacity to see and to hope in the profound goodness of man when others are unable to do so or are overcome by skepticism, by keeping faith in human life, etc. Faith, in the order and goodness of reality, in the attainability of the ideal, in the possibility of justice, truth and liberty—this faith is the only way in which Christians can give witness to Christianity, that is, the Incarnation of Jesus, son of God, and the presence of the Spirit of God on the earth.[6]

It is for this type of presence that pastoral action must work to match our times. Since socialization is restructuring society with associational forms which are neither voluntary nor free, the action of Christian groups should be geared to this fact. The effectiveness of pastoral action will thus be proved, not only by the affirmation and recognition of the corporate rights of the Christian group or of the Church, as if these were detached from the world and uninterested in its destiny, but by the inspiration, the leaven, it succeeds in giving to the entire growth of the human world.

The basic organism in which the Christian works to generate and regenerate mankind is still the family cell. Pastoral attention to the family—which may be said to have come into being with the very plan of God, in Eden with the creation of the first couple, in the Redemption with the presence of Christ in humanity through the family in Nazareth —is also to be adapted to the modern situation.

As the family ceases to be the basic unit of production—or

in a certain sense, of consumption—its values relate rather to employment, access to spiritual and cultural benefits, and "holy" leisure. This transformation of the earthly context of the human couple has for many years furthered in the Church a new type of spirituality in which the elements of choice and the values of the body, freed from the pressures of elementary need, have the ascendancy over those elements and values determined by the circumstances created by poverty. Freer discussion of sex and family relations, the problem of national birth control, the crisis in parental authority, the trend away from the "institution" concept of the family to that of the "contractual," are merely the social expressions of this inversion in the hierarchy of family values. However much it is conditioned by biological factors and—according to cultural anthropology—by the circumscribed environment in which it finds itself, the modern family nevertheless is established, lives its life, and develops in greater freedom, which is marked by a certain air of crisis and bewilderment only because of a lack of psychological maturity and more solid social guarantees.

This is where pastoral action must find its strong point, for in the consolidation of new attitudes and behavior with the ethical center lies the possibility of influence which is not confined to preserving the old idealized values of the Christian family. Pastoral action must match the factors which exert varying pressures on the situation and must be guided by the existential circumstances and anthropological exigencies (e.g., the diversity of ethical imperatives which different family situations produce depending on the average family size, the

housing situation, the access to schools and recreation, the way
the household is organized in particular traditions or areas).
The particular aspects of the moral law to be emphasized and
the specific elements of family spirituality to be indicated with
greater relevance can be determined precisely on the basis of
knowledge of all such variations. This predicates a constant
rethinking of practical theology, the definite abandonment
of a system of individualistic precepts, and an appreciation of
family values and their more knowledgeable insertion—all
in the framework of modern man's religious values.

The action taken by the Council and the widespread sensitivity it created should reach all pastoral action. But progress
in the area of the family unit will be the slowest. In the
course of time, family life and sexual behavior have been over-
laid with encrustations of individualistic puritanism, and to
extricate them without giving the impression of yielding to
a current and widespread form of license will be very difficult. Yet difficulty is both the test and proof of the sound-
ness of the Church's action in the world.

Modern society is, or is about to be, a society of affluence,
pervaded by the idea of progress. The reason for treating, in
earlier chapters of the present volume, the evolution of two
key concepts of today's world was not to list the variations
they have undergone but to discover the points of leverage
they offer for the action which the Church must accomplish
in the world. Modern man is imbued with the idea of progress. Leaving aside definitions of progress, which recall the
adage that "there are as many opinions as there are heads,"
the fact remains that competition and success are values that

animate and agitate man today. In the whole gamut of social symbols of status and power, it may be noted that abstract and concrete definitions of both are always related to personal and social success, considered most of the time as justification in itself for the entire life of an individual, a group, or a nation. In other words, the explosion of affluence resulting from the scientific-technological revolution has created a sense of excitement in individuals and groups which cancels out, deadens, or at least reduces the values of communion and sharing with others. The Promethean tension of that state of mind has often been stressed, but too little consideration has been given this painless denial of the interior aspects of community life. Similarly, attention has been rightly transferred from the alienation due to nonownership of property to that deriving from nonparticipation in power or in its legitimation or exercise. But, again, not much attention has been given to the weakening of the social motivations induced by and directed toward a philosophy of consumption—due to an ironclad automatic law of dependence on production. There has been recurrent moralizing on the subject and a great deal of abstract talk about revision and reform, but all of this has nothing whatever to do with the concrete life of human groups.

Now, precisely because the Christian concepts of man postulate the management of science and technology for social ends, it is possible—in this surge of progress, which frees and elevates man, broadening his possibilities for being and for self-expression—for Christianity to animate those values of community and sharing for which it is the source and which have a much stronger and more enduring motivational charge than the philosophy of progress and consumption. The Church's pastoral activity, therefore, should tend to undertake an internal evaluation of progress and well-being, accepting them as human activity but pointing out their limitations and introducing the ethical imperatives of solidarity. This means that pastoral action must tend to a rigor and strictness that measures responsibilities by something much higher and greater than moralistic bickerings—by God himself, who is the final end of history.

The new understanding of poverty is, I believe, to be viewed in this context. Traditionally, apart from the vows of religious through the centuries, poverty has been associated with certain needy situations. Today, with the abundance of goods in an affluent society and the exaltation of the human ego due to the prodigies of science and technology, it is given a much more voluntary aspect. In other words, slavery to the myth of the unending cycle of production and consumer goods cannot be overcome except through spiritual purification of the means of man's action in the world and the independent choice of a state or mode of life in which poverty is the inner victor against the automatic pressures of expanding production. Though the thrust of development will indeed have to be maintained, instead of making the acquisition of greater material well-being within a competitive economy the ultimate value of labor and of family, other values may be introduced as a kind of conscience-governed filter. This would entail renunciation or reduction of certain areas of choice which, while they lead to wealth, deprive the individual of his chief characteristic as a human being, namely, autonomy in the choice of his own destiny and the way in which he will pursue it. Analysis of the process by which a society achieves general prosperity, study of the desirable and proximate conditions of full employment with the accompanying problems of increased individual income and spending power and of reaction to the automatic expansion of a consumption-oriented civilization are indispensable for arriving at a moral judgment on prosperity in general and for eliciting ethical-ascetic responsibility in the choice of means which translate it into reality. In addition to its ascetic value, elective poverty could be for the Christian a form of witness. It would mean that he renounces certain goods in order to be more independent as a man, that he renounces them in order to affirm the superior value of the riches God communicates to him, that he renounces them because of the historic opportunity for solidarity with the countries of the "third world" in their pursuit of human freedoms.

For pastoral action with this aim, it is assumed that the Church, as a social organism, will serve as an example in the choice and use of means for action, give up its privileges, and make sure that no traces of imperialism or Caesaropapism remain in its style, language, outward dress, or dialogue with the world. In essence, this means nothing other than choosing a way of life and using the goods of this world without becoming enslaved by them. The ministry is service, *diaconia,* the solicitous awakening of the torpid areas in the human conscience, a recall to the ideal and to the discipline of responsibility, independently of the means which life places at one's disposal and which are more effective for one's personal pursuits.

The problems concerning quantity-quality and the elite-mass relationships, debated so much by clergy and scholars, are irrelevant; the important thing for pastoral action to achieve is the growth of the collective conscience and of solidary action. The first contact for the action of the ecclesiastical structure and culture in the world should be, for every man of good will, an entreaty to his conscience, an appeal to his full humanity. There are no special times, no distinctions as to race or society, which can nullify the concrete value of such an entreaty and appeal. The Church is not called upon to solve all the problems of this world—although, unfortunately, a certain importance has been attached to this in some circles. But the Church is called upon to offer its service of the Word, to be ready to assist all that man is achieving or trying to achieve to improve his lot, to inspire human history, to make it a sacred history. And the Church is all of us; we are all called upon to make history sacred, that is, to fulfil ourselves through a divine vocation which weaves through and illumines all our earthly labors. It is in this profound action at the heart of history that the Church maintains its identity, while it alters its structures, assimilates the unceasing accomplishments of human genius, and adapts its action and mechanisms to the ever-changing setting of earthly vicissitudes.

The most obvious conclusion of this perspective is that the Church, being the consciousness of the historic Christ in the faith, is clearly the consciousness of the world and cosmos, revealing their inner unity, a unity which is ever assailed by evil and the forces of deterioration, but which is always rediscovered and affirmed in love. The Church changes with the world, offering to the world the knowledge of its final destiny, which encompasses all human labors, all of history. It may be said, in a certain sense, that only the Church changes profoundly because it has an identity, while the world changes because it is groping for its identity without ever fully discovering it.

The essential task of the Church is not so much to judge as to grasp the meaning of the world's journey, through and beyond its expression in the separate historic realities of specific regions and specific times. Only after it has grasped this meaning does the Church interpret its direct relationship to the perennial travail of all the universe seeking to express itself in a new creation.

Notes

[1] F. Houtart, L. Grond, C. Thoen, "L'Eglise et l'Aide aux Pays en Voie de Developpement," in *Les Dossiers de l'Action Sociale Catholique,* No. 6 (1962), p. 11; also, "Development Aid by Christian Lay Groups," in *Pro Mundi Vita,* No. 5 (1965), especially pp. 29–39.

[2] See Chapter 3, "Function and Mechanism of Adaptation."

[3] It is in this context that the term is used in the encyclical *Mater et Magistra.*

[4] See, especially, Chapter 3.

[5] E. Pin, "Les Instituts Religieux Apostoliques et le Changement Socioculturel," in *Nouvelle Revue Théologique,* No. 4 (1965), pp. 395–411.

[6] F. Balbo, "Scriti Inediti di F. Balbo," in *La Revista Trimestrale,* Nos. 11–12 (1964), pp. 697–698.